The Biblical Seminar
68

WHY ARE YOU
SILENT, LORD?

WHY ARE YOU SILENT, LORD?

Roman Garrison

Sheffield Academic Press

This work is dedicated in memory of Nancy Hall,
Peter Macky, Bardarah McCandless, Tom and Jean McCracken
and Bill George

Copyright © 2000 Sheffield Academic Press

Published by
Sheffield Academic Press Ltd
Mansion House
19 Kingfield Road
Sheffield S11 9AS
England

Typeset by Sheffield Academic Press
and
Printed on acid-free paper in Great Britain
by Biddles Ltd
Guildford, Surrey

British Library Cataloguing in Publication Data

A catalogue record for this book is available
from the British Library

ISBN 1-84127-069-5

CONTENTS

PREFACE

Martin Hengel, in his research on the theme of innocent suffering in the context of the general idea of atonement, raised the question whether such a concept is in fact distinctively 'Jewish'. He comments

> Any historical investigation which is to do justice to the New Testament cannot be content with stressing the tradition of the Old Testament and Judaism, important though that may be; it must also pay very close attention to the Graeco-Roman world, where the problems become particularly interesting at the point where Jewish and Greek conceptions have already become fused in the pre-Christian period.[1]

The present analysis, as a response to Hengel's observation, is largely an attempt, within the discipline of New Testament studies, to treat an emotional and frightening question in a manner in which the researcher can achieve a small measure of objectivity. The problems labeled 'theodicy' arise not only as a theological and historical concern. The issue has also become personal to me through the suffering and deaths of special friends and family members. It is to their memory that this book is dedicated.

I gratefully acknowledge the tireless and generous contributions, through discussion and gentle but firm criticism, of Dr Hilton Turner. He was kind enough to read several rough drafts of my work and patiently offered insights and suggestions. At the risk of folly I have sometimes chosen not to heed his advice. For those errors I bear full responsibility.

Most translations of texts are my own unless indicated, and perhaps some readers will object that I am 'too loose' with the material I have chosen to present. The argument certainly has merit, and if I gave priority to literalness as a measure of accuracy in translation, I would be repentant. Of greater importance to me, however, is to capture the ever

---

1. Martin Hengel, *The Atonement* (Philadelphia: Fortress Press, 1981), p. 5.

elusive sense of the passage that underlies the words. To the charge of subjectivity I would then plead guilty, but my hope is that some in the courtroom will at least believe that my motivation was worthwhile.

INTRODUCTION

> Not only is life brief, but further there is no one on earth who is so happy
> as never to wish to be dead rather than alive. Such a thought occurs not
> just once but often in one's lifetime. People are trampled by tragic events
> and illness that make life seem long. Consequently, people look forward
> to death as a desirable escape from a trouble-plagued life. This demon-
> strates the god's envy in that we have just begun to taste the sweetness of
> life (Herodotus 7.46).

No rational and compassionate individual who has visited a ward in a
hospital for children could seriously maintain that we live in 'the best
of all possible worlds'.[1] A belief in the supreme deity of Judaism and
Christianity (or in the justice of Zeus or Jupiter) is most forcefully chal-
lenged by the problem of evil. It has been claimed with clear justification: 'Theodicy has always been the most difficult task of any
monotheistic theology assuming the omnipotence and benevolence of
the God'.[2]

'Theodicy' is the attempt to reconcile or account for the existence of
evil with the presumed wisdom and fairness of the Master of the universe. Its etymological roots are found in the Greek words for 'god' and
'justice'; and the theological paradox was a source of anxiety in the
ancient world.[3] Although ancient Greek popular religion is polytheistic
and the immortals are basically amoral beings, throughout Greek literature, nevertheless, there is the 'consistent presence' of this issue of
theodicy. This concern is given expression by Theognis, in whose

---

1.   Cf. Diogenes Allen's comment in the Introduction to Gottfried Wilhelm
Leibniz, *Theodicy* (trans. E.M. Huggard; ed. and abridged by Diogenes Allen; Don
Mills, ON: Bobbs-Merrill Co. Inc., 1966), p. vii.

2.   Jeffrey Burton Russell, *Satan* (Ithaca: Cornell University Press, 1981), p. 17;
cf. John Hick, *Evil and the God of Love* (Norfolk: Macmillan and Co., 1966), p. 4.

3.   Hick, *Evil*, p. 6; William Chase Greene, *Moira* (New York: Harper and
Row, 1944), p. 5.

writing one discovers 'an important stage in Greek religious thought, in which the justice of Zeus was being seriously questioned'.[4]

> You surprise me dear Zeus! You are the omnipresent lord, holding all power and tremendous honor. You have knowledge of every mortal heart and mind. Your kingly rule is unchallenged in the whole world. How then, son of Cronos, can you bear it to see both criminals and honest people, thoughtful and moderate mortals as well as weak sinners, share in the identical fate?[5]

Within Judaism, theodicy has long been a significant concern. Quite recently, Harold S. Kushner, in his popular *When Bad Things Happen to Good People*, has claimed that theologians (and all people of mono-theistic faith) must surrender the conviction that God is omnipotent in order to maintain the hope that God at least cares about those who suffer. He argues that, like the author of the book of Job,[6] he prefers to believe in the goodness of God. 'If God is a God of justice and not of power, then He can still be on our side when bad things happen to us.'[7] Kushner's central thesis is that 'Fate, not God, sends us the problem'.[8] The many theological ramifications of this suggestion need not distract us.

The Christian theologian, Augustine, wrote a comprehensive treatment of the issue and attempted to affirm the justice of God while acknowledging the undeniable misery of those thought to be God's children. Augustine, maintaining a fatalistic attitude, however, rejoiced that temporal evils could not exist independent of the will of God. 'Though it be objected that Christians have been killed or ravaged by hideous diseases, if this must be grieved over still it is the fate shared by all who live (Augustine, *The City of God* 1.11).' While several perspectives are possible and do or at least can inform an understanding of the problem, questions remain.

---

4.   Hesiod, *Hesiod and Theognis* (Introduction and Translation by Dorothea Wender: Harmondsworth: Penguin Books, 1973), p. 90.

5.   Theognis, *Elegies*, pp. 373-79.

6.   Harold S. Kushner, *When Bad Things Happen to Good People* (New York: Schocken Books, 1981), p. 43.

7.   Kushner, *Bad Things*, p. 44.

8.   Kushner, *Bad Things*, pp. 46, 129. Cf. Greene, *Moira*, p. 3: 'Shall we set Fate above God?'

The central concern of this book is the problem of innocent suffering in the Greek, Roman and biblical traditions.[9] My study is the product of two concerns, one academic and one personal. As an intellectual theme, the issue of the relationship between the determining will of God and individual freedom has long intrigued me and involved me in several debates about the goodness of God and about human responsibility for certain choices or actions, particularly where they involve the suffering of righteous (or pious) people.

One of my attempts to address the problem of 'destiny' is in my essay, 'Legions of Angels and the Will of God' where I briefly compare the decision-to-die made by Achilles, Socrates, Jesus (in Matthew's Gospel), and Ignatius of Antioch.[10] Each affirms the role of fate (or God's intention) *and* the significance of human decision in the ending of life, including those situations where death appears unjust. The problem, however, does not allow for easy analysis and such a comparison is only a small contribution to the dialogue.

The discussion of theodicy has been echoed and amplified in many classrooms where I have taught courses on the biblical literature. In reading through the so-called Minor Prophets, I have drawn attention to Amos 3.6 ('Does disaster strike a city apart from God causing it?'), and I have asked students how they would answer that question using contemporary examples: 'If a hurricane destroys a city in Florida and hundreds of people die in the storm, is God responsible for the tragedy?' The variety of responses has been fascinating.

The mocking words of Lucian as he challenges Zeus, combined with the protest of the Psalms in confronting Yahweh, provided the eventual title of this work: *Why are you Silent, Lord?*[11] It seemed to me a worthwhile project broadly to study the theme of innocent suffering, and the implicit theodicy, in the Greek, the Roman and the biblical traditions.

9. Cf. Charles H. Talbert, *Learning through Suffering* (Collegeville, MN: Liturgical Press, 1991), p. 11: 'Early Christianity had Jewish roots and developed in a context that was not only Jewish but also Greco-Roman. Consequently, in order to discern the contours of an early Christian position on suffering it is helpful, indeed necessary, to view it against the background of how suffering was interpreted by ancient Judaism and in the Greco-Roman tradition.'

10. Found in Roman Garrison, *The Graeco-Roman Context of Early Christian Literature* (Sheffield: Sheffield Academic Press, 1998).

11. Lucian, *Zeus Catechized* 16; Ps. 28.1; 35.22; 109.1 (cf. Isa. 64.12).

At the same time as I, in my ivory tower, wrestled with this idea, several of my friends and relatives outside the castle were enduring tremendous suffering. This has had the effect of turning intellectual curiosity into a genuine hunger for knowledge and understanding. With a sense of dread and urgency, I seek for myself an answer to the cry that each might have uttered, 'My God, my God, why have you forsaken me?' How can Christianity proclaim the love and power of God in the shadow of pain? Still, the Apostle Paul seems well aware of the irony or paradox when he writes, 'Who is able to separate us from Christ's love? Tribulation, anxiety, persecution, starvation, nakedness, danger, or violent death? ... No, in all these things we are more than conquerors through the one who loved us (Rom. 8.35, 37).

Yet the 'why' remains. Like the torments of Heracles, this question often disturbs those who try to sleep. In the following pages, attention is given to several figures, in fiction and history, who have suffered undeservedly and to the variety of their attitudes or responses to their situation and to the issues involved.

First, I survey broadly the problem of innocent suffering in Greek, Roman and biblical traditions in order to introduce the problem of innocent suffering as a theme which permeates ancient literature and history. In the second chapter I give more specific attention to the characters of Hector and Sarpedon in the *Iliad*. The epic claims that piety is often rewarded by the gods, and it is consistently maintained that parents, divine and human, are concerned for the well-being of their children. Yet the pious Hector and Zeus' son Sarpedon are both killed in battle with the clear foreknowledge and acquiescence of the immortals.

The third chapter contains an examination of the Heracles tradition as found in Euripides and Sophocles. In their plays once again the suffering and death of a son of Zeus are set in deliberate contrast against a background where parental affection for children is stressed.

Chapter 4 focuses on the character of Socrates and the differing perspectives of Xenophon and Plato. Both, however, regard Socrates as an individual 'made perfect', either as an inspiration or an example to others, and this theme of perfectability becomes especially prominent in the biblical tradition of Wisdom of Solomon and Hebrews.

The fifth chapter gives consideration to Musonius Rufus, Epictetus and Seneca, the Roman Stoics. In their teaching the ideas that suffering or hardship is like athletic training for the Olympic contest of life and that perfection might be achieved through invincibility are significant because the metaphors are appropriated in *4 Maccabees* and early Christian literature.

In Chapter 6, the portrait of pious sufferers in Wisdom of Solomon draws together several of the themes from previous chapters: the suffering of God's children even in a context where parental love (of human beings) is stressed, the hope of becoming perfect, and the athletic struggle of pain and affliction. Further, Wisdom of Solomon, adopting an interpretation from the Hebrew Scriptures, emphatically regards suffering as evidence that God is testing or disciplining his children. This motif is especially significant in the tradition about Jesus and in the New Testament epistle to the Hebrews (which are central topics in Chapter 7). The letter gives evidence to support Hengel's claim: 'the problems become particularly interesting at the point where Jewish and Greek conceptions have already become fused in the pre-Christian period'.[12]

While my principal interest is a literary comparison, the theological understanding is an overwhelming concern. It is my hope that through a study of the themes in these sources, we may gain insight into the purpose of God in the several instances of innocent suffering, that a glimmer of hope might shine on the dark 'why?'.

12. Hengel, *The Atonement*, p. 5.

Chapter 1

Innocent Suffering in the Greek, Roman and Biblical Traditions

(O LORD) Your eyes are too holy to see evil and you are not able to look on sin. Why, then, do you see the treacherous and yet are silent when the wicked consume those who are more righteous? (Hab. 1.13).

1. *Introduction*

In Sophocles' famous play, Oedipus wished Creon well with bitter words: 'May Providence be kinder to you than it has been to me', (Sophocles, *Oedipus the King* 1478-79). Lucian, the satirist and virtual philosopher of the second century CE, once asked why the wicked so often are happy and comfortable while the good are frequently persecuted, stricken with disease and impoverished (Lucian, *Zeus Catechized* 17; cf. *Zeus Rants* 19). Seneca calmly acknowledged the sad reality: 'Innocent people sometimes die. Who could deny that? (Seneca, *Moral Epistles* 14.15). In the Greek, Roman and biblical traditions there is a shared anxiety regarding the injustice and apparent inevitability of pious individuals experiencing the so-called 'natural' torments associated with the human condition. Philosophy became intensely personal at the approach of death when the emperor Titus objected that it was unfair that life should be taken from him 'since but one sin weighed on his conscience' (Suetonius, *Titus* 10).

Seemingly in defiance of conventional wisdom, Plato had insisted that the just (*ho dikaios*) *ought* to anticipate misery and undeserved suffering (Plato, *Republic* 361E). Furthermore, to some interpreters, even the death of Socrates seemed to sanction the idea that the gods worked their purpose even through the death of the innocent (Xenophon, *Apology*). Perhaps this viewpoint emerged as an attempt to explain the existence of evil in a universe controlled by the Divine.

Suffering, however, in a world governed by God—and all the more

when the god is characterized as love or *agapē* (1 Jn 4.8, 16)—is indeed
a scandal[1] but the pain, deprivation, and anguish of the *innocent* is even
more problematic, especially for biblical theology.[2] Boethius confronted this crisis not as an intellectual hurdle but as a personal concern.
Languishing in prison, tortured by the injustice of his plight, he wrestled with the question of God's Providence.

> And then Philosophy said, 'Do you think that this world is governed
> merely by random chance? Or do you instead believe that it is ruled by
> reason?'
> 'I cannot imagine', I said, 'that such events are caused simply by chance.
> And I am certain that God the Creator rules over his work. I shall never
> be distracted from that judgment' (Boethius, *The Consolation of Philos-
> ophy* 1.6.5-11).[3]

Theodicy has been a vital issue for human beings throughout the
history of thought.[4] It finds implicit expression in Greek, Roman and
biblical portraits of the lives of the pious (including those who are identified as the children of God) who have suffered despite their apparent
righteousness. This first chapter will explore the general theme of theodicy as it is found in the stories of literary and historical characters in
the Graeco-Roman and biblical worlds: Hippolytus, Nicias, Aeneas,
Marcus Aurelius, Job and Jesus.[5] Each of these individuals could be
seen as an 'innocent victim'. I will give attention to how the events that
shaped these separate tragedies were understood in the context of the
belief that control of all that happens is in the hands of God (or the
gods) (Sophocles, *Oedipus at Colonus* 1443-44).

2. *Greek Characters*

a. *Literary*
The issues related to theodicy haunt Greek culture. Even in the opening
lines of the *Iliad*, Homer acknowledged the bitter paradox that the

---

1. Peter Kreeft, *Making Sense Out of Suffering* (Ann Arbor: Servant Books,
1986), p. 17; cf. John Hick, *Evil and the God of Love* (Norfolk: Macmillan and Co.,
1966), p. ix.
2. Sam K. Williams, *Jesus' Death as Saving Event* (Missoula, MT: Scholars
Press, 1975), p. 93.
3. For an evaluation of Boethius's work, see Kreeft, *Making Sense*, p. 65.
4. Again for this term, see Hick, *Evil and the God of Love*, p. 6.
5. Hick, *Evil and the God of Love*, p. 279.

deaths of many Greek soldiers in the last battles of the Trojan War were not only the indirect result of Achilles' anger but were, at another level, more directly a fulfillment of the will and purpose of Zeus (*Iliad* 1.1-5). The apparent injustice that the evil and the good would share a similar fate evoked protest from the poets (again, see Theognis, *Elegies* 373-79; cf. Eccles. 8.14). This concern continually echoes in Greek literature and is especially prominent in the plays of Euripides.

The comic dramatist Aristophanes mockingly charged Euripides with virtual atheism (Aristophanes, *Thesmophoriazusae* 450-51), an accusation seemingly grounded in the latter playwright's hostile attitude toward the behavior of the gods and goddesses in his works. Some scholars insist, however, that while 'Euripides may lay open mythological gods to criticism, he finds no fault with, indeed he supports, the fundamental beliefs and practices of popular religion'.[6]

Regardless of Euripides' personal theology, it is indisputable that the immortal characters in many of his plays are responsible for the suffering (and death) of innocent people. One such righteous 'victim' is Hippolytus in the work named for him, its chief character. Aphrodite, who resents Hippolytus for his rejection of her, tortures the young man both physically and emotionally. Yet she also, if grudgingly, admits his innocence as she acknowledges that he is pure-hearted (*agnou*).[7]

In *Hippolytus* the central character is consistently portrayed as pious, devoted to the worship of and fellowship with Artemis. He is often referred to as a god-fearing individual.[8] In Hippolytus's single-minded reverence there is no room for the pleasures of sexuality. In his rejection of physical intimacy, Hippolytus not only denounces women in general (*Hippolytus* 616-68), but Aphrodite in particular (*Hippolytus* 12-13; 21-22; 106-107). As a consequence, Aphrodite despises Hippolytus and plans his destruction, even though another innocent victim will die in his being 'punished' (*Hippolytus* 46-50).[9]

Through Aphrodite's power and influence, Phaedra, the stepmother of Hippolytus, is consumed by a physical desire for the young man. Her

---

6.   Jon D. Mikalson, *Honor Thy Gods* (Chapel Hill: University of North Carolina Press, 1991), p. 236.

7.   *Hippolytus* 11; cf. early Christian usage of the term in 2 Cor. 7.11; 1 Jn 3.3; 2 Clem. 6.9.

8.   *Hippolytus* 656; 993-96; 1060-61. Cf. Jn 9.31.

9.   Cf. Hazel E. Barnes, *Hippolytus in Drama and Myth* (Lincoln: University of Nebraska Press, 1960), p. 73.

nurse apparently asks him to take an oath of silence and seeks to explain her mistress's need to Hippolytus. He repudiates any thought of such a union, and in utter degradation (and shame), Phaedra commits suicide. She leaves a note, however, accusing Hippolytus of raping her.

Theseus, the father of Hippolytus and the husband of Phaedra, discovers his wife's corpse and on reading the message she has left, is filled with rage, contempt and even vengeful hatred for his son. Theseus asks Poseidon to execute Hippolytus and in the event that the god will not heed this prayer, Theseus decides to exile the alleged offender, driving him from his *polis*.[10]

As Hippolytus prepares to leave his home and readies his chariot, Poseidon sends a great monster from the sea that attacks and indirectly wounds the young man. Dying, Hippolytus is brought before Theseus, and a messenger insists that the victim is innocent.[11] Theseus is nevertheless convinced of his son's guilt until Artemis herself appears and confronts the father. She accuses him of murdering his righteous son. While the goddess grieves that Hippolytus is near death, she is either unable or unwilling to restore him.

The innocence and piety of Hippolytus are consistently maintained throughout the tragedy. Aphrodite does not punish him for a specific crime; she only seeks out of vanity to destroy the one who rejects her, an attitude which she personally regards as virtual blasphemy (*Hippolytus* 1-13; 21-22). Theseus, while denouncing his son as guilty, ironically testifies to the young man's apparent virtue (*Hippolytus* 948-50). Artemis, defending Hippolytus's reputation even as he dies, says to Theseus: 'I have come to show that your son's heart was always innocent and he dies for his good name... Because of his piety he did not fall in with her [i.e. Phaedra] nor break his oath when you reviled him.'[12]

Significantly, Hippolytus himself protests the injustice of his suffering, but he calls out to Zeus, not Artemis. He complains that his piety and chastity, even his worship of the gods, have been meaningless in light of the undeserved misery the immortals have brought on him (*Hippolytus* 1363-69).

---

10. *Hippolytus* 892-98. Discovering later that his prayer was in fact answered, Theseus cries out, 'Poseidon, you are truly my father', 1169-70.

11. *Hippolytus* 1249-54. Cf. the centurion's 'verdict' in Lk. 23.47.

12. Hippolytus 1298-1309. Theseus, grieving for his son, cries, 'Woe for your goodness, piety, and virtue' (line 1454).

Two of the nurse's lines bring out the implicit theodicy of the play:

> All of us must at some time suffer for we are mortal (*Hippolytus* 207).

> Aphrodite, you are not simply a goddess. You are stronger than a god if that can be (*Hippolytus* 359-60).

In Hippolytus, Euripides stressed that the sexual nature of human beings and, within mythology, of many of the gods and goddesses is so powerful as to subject these persons to forces that often lead to suffering. Yet resistance is foolish and may result in death. Because the myths suggest that even Zeus can be mastered by Aphrodite and the sexual urge, the gods are ultimately unable or unwilling to prevent that suffering. At most, vengeance against Aphrodite might be planned (cf. *Hippolytus* 1416-19).

If Euripides were asked about the purpose of the gods in having Hippolytus suffer even though he was innocent of any crime, he might have replied that the character's fate was not the result of an intelligent Providence but the tragic consequence of his personal goodness within an evil world. To some degree Plato would agree that personal goodness or virtue is often destroyed by human frailty.

b. *Historical*

According to Thucydides, the Peloponnesian War was the most significant event in the history of Greece up to the time when he wrote. Consequently, he chose to give it special attention as the subject of his historical account (Thucydides 1.1). Among the individuals who lived during that period, Aristotle identifies Thucydides as one of the most patriotic, virtuous and statesmanlike—one of the best politicians—in Athens. The only other person to share with Thucydides in Aristotle's praise of character and achievement was Nicias (Aristotle, *Constitution of Athens* 28.5).

Nicias is best known for his efforts in arranging a truce in the Peloponnesian War. This brief halt to the conflict came to be called 'The Peace of Nicias'.[13] In Plutarch's *Nicias*, however, a more prominent theme in the biography of the man is his piety and righteousness. These qualities in Nicias provoke the questions related to theodicy.

---

13. For an excellent survey and description, see Donald Kagan, *The Peace of Nicias and the Sicilian Expedition* (Ithaca, NY: Cornell University Press, 1981).

In a fair amount of detail, Plutarch describes Nicias as a man of goodness and discretion (*Nicias* 532),[14] notes that both his sources and even the architecture that has survived to his day suggest that Nicias sacrificed to the gods daily (*Nicias* 524-25), and reports that the people of Athens said that he was 'god-loved' (*theophilēs*).[15] Furthermore, it was believed that because of his exceptional piety Nicias was granted by Providence to lend his name to the truce that interrupted the Peloponnesian War. As Pericles was thought by the people to be responsible for the hostilities, Nicias was thought to be the principal reason for the peace (*Nicias* 529).

For Nicias to endure suffering was not only unexpected, it was, in fact, alarming. When, in a later military campaign, Nicias's forces endured considerable misery, it was anticipated that the immortals would intervene on behalf of Nicias. In the midst of his anguish he could say

> I have spent my life performing the religious duties towards the gods and just, even blameless, service for mortals. Consequently, despite the present misfortunes, I am not frightened as I might be. Instead I am confident in my hope for the future (Thucydides 7.77.2-3).

Nicias's expectations were not realized and he died in misery. Thucydides comments that such a person 'was the least deserving of such disaster' (Thucydides 7.86.5). Plutarch as well observed that Nicias's suffering was 'undeserved' (*Nicias* 540) and refers to the disheartened reaction of the soldiers who witnessed the tragedy. Their conviction—that piety and righteousness, at least scrupulous religiosity, would guarantee the favor of the gods—was destroyed.

> They had no reason to hope for assistance from the gods when they saw a person as god-loved [*theophilēs*][16] as Nicias, someone who had performed many great and lavish religious duties, had met with no better fortune than the most insignificant member of the army (Plutarch, *Nicias* 540).

Although neither Thucydides nor Plutarch attempt to explain the tragedy of Nicias within a framework of theodicy, Plutarch would likely have accounted for undeserved suffering with a near-Stoic toler-

---

14. For an interesting comparison of *chrēstou*, see Tertullian, *Apology* 3.5.

15. Cf. Lk. 1.3; Acts 1.1. Cf. the comment by Mikalson, *Honor thy Gods*, p. 163.

16. See n. 36.

ance of the unpredictability of Providence. In his letter of condolence to a grieving friend he wrote:

> The counsel of the Pythagoreans is magnificent: Whatever misery mortals suffer by the gods' dispensation, whatever fate you must endure, bear it without indignation (*A Letter of Condolence to Apollonius* 116 E, F; *Carmina Aurea* 17).

Plato's later warning, certainly the product of his knowledge of Socrates' trial and execution, that the truly good individual would suffer, seems well-rooted in Greek literature and an awareness of Greek history. Within their literary context Hippolytus and Nicias illustrate the frightening reality that the innocent often endure undeserved misery.[17] Greek thought regarded the evil that befalls the righteous as capricious, almost haphazard, and an inescapable aspect of life itself.

3. *Roman Characters*

a. *Literary*

In Virgil's *Aeneid*, the protagonist 'had a character already well established by literature and legend'.[18] Aeneas has a fairly significant role in the *Iliad* where he is the son of Aphrodite and one of the heroic Trojan warriors.

In the *Iliad*, Aeneas is almost killed on two separate occasions but is rescued from harm by the immortals. Aphrodite (with Apollo's help) intervenes to save her son from death at the hands of Diomedes (*Iliad* 5.310-45). When Achilles himself is preparing to kill Aeneas, Poseidon, the sea-god, miraculously spares the life of the intended victim. This god is motivated by a compassion which shows an awareness of Aeneas's 'destiny' and an overwhelming appreciation for his piety.

> With his sword Achilles was about to rob Aeneas of life, but Poseidon, Shaker of Earth, saw what might happen. He spoke to the other gods, 'Behold, I feel grief for magnanimous Aeneas who will soon go down to Hades, slain by Achilles... Yet why should he, a guiltless [*anaitios*; cf. Mt. 12.5, 7] man, suffer for reasons not related to him? Furthermore, he constantly offers gifts to the gods of heaven. No, let us lead him out of death so that Zeus will not be angry that Achilles killed him. For it is ordained for him to escape (*Iliad* 20.290-302).

17. Mikalson, *Honor thy Gods*, p. 163.
18. Nicolas Moseley, *Characters and Epithets* (New Haven: Yale University Press, 1926), p. 68.

Indeed, Aeneas escaped Troy as it was being overrun by the Greeks. In the Roman version of his legend he journeyed on to found the civilization that would be known as the Roman Empire. The epic which describes his mission is the *Aeneid*. While the story continues to stress the piety and courage of the hero, his considerable suffering and anguish become the more dominant themes. Aphrodite (= Venus) protests to Zeus (= Jupiter) the injustice of her son's plight: 'Did my Aeneas commit some great crime?'(*Aeneid* 1.231). Following the religious tradition inherited from Homer, Virgil attributed the pitiable condition of his protagonist to the malicious anger of Hera (= Juno).[19] The author then asked the muse that inspired him: 'How can such fierce resentment abide in the heart of a goddess?' (*Aeneid* 1.8-11).

Aeneas endures much misery from the *Iliad* to the *Aeneid*. Perhaps none is so great as that which results from the death of his wife, Creusa, whom he lost the night Troy was destroyed. Weary with grief, Aeneas bitterly recalls that continually he groaned as he cried out for the woman he loved (*Aeneid* 2.731-51, 769).

Having the opportunity to develop a relationship with another woman for whom he felt considerable affection, Aeneas was once more forced by fate to be separated from his love. Despite his intense feeling for Dido and the luxurious life available to him with her, Aeneas left her as he resumed his mission. Virgil comments, 'even as his heart sighed and his love for her shook him, still he accepted heaven's course and went back to his shipmates' (*Aeneid* 4.393-96). In utter despair Dido commits suicide. Aeneas is tormented by his apparent responsibility for her death. Seeing her in the underworld, the land of the dead, he calls out, 'Was I the cause of your death?' (*Aeneid* 6.458). Aeneas must then bear her silent rejection.

If even Poseidon was unwilling that a guiltless man like Aeneas should know pain and endure suffering, if Aphrodite could object to the unfairness of Aeneas's misery, then what purpose can be given to his story? The most likely, though theologically unsatisfying, answer is perhaps found in the nationalistic interest of the author. Virgil, although sympathetic to his protagonist, was describing his misfortune to illustrate that individual travail was necessary for the emergence of the Roman Empire. World history was more significant than the personal

---

19. In this way, Aeneas parallels Heracles! See Chapter 3.

contentment of any individual, and such was the will and intention of Zeus (= Jupiter).[20]

b. *Historical*

Marcus Aurelius was regarded as one of the most, if not *the* most pious of the Roman emperors. Julius Capitolinus, in his tribute, acknowledged that following the man's death Marcus was believed to be 'a god'.[21] The piety of Marcus was apparently admitted by Christian witnesses, including Justin Martyr (cf. *First Apology* 1-2). Dio Cassius praised him as 'consistently pure, magnificent, and god-fearing *(eusebes)*' (Dio, *Roman History* 72.30.2; 72.34.2). The ancient historian went on to chronicle the achievements of Marcus and offered the following analysis: 'he did not receive the good fortune of which he was worthy' (Dio, *Roman History* 72.36.3).

The *Meditations* of Marcus Aurelius certainly testify to his intention to be reverent and blameless. Throughout the work the author counsels the reader:

> The deity within you ought to have jurisdiction over one who is energetic and mature, a statesman, a Roman, a king (Marcus Aurelius, *Meditations* 3.5).

> Live with the gods and demonstrate for them a soul that is at peace with what they give. Such is the will of the deity within you, even that part of Zeus himself given to all, to rule and to guide, that is, the mind (*Meditations* 5.27).

> Even though you might not be recognised, it is certainly possible to be godlike (*Meditations* 7.67).

From the *Meditations*, one would expect the emperor to have accepted (stoically) any adversity as providential, even willed by the gods.[22] Sadly, such a highly regarded, perhaps righteous, individual was subject to the grief and torment brought on by the deaths of his wife and several of his children, the outbreak of the plague in the capital city, a civil war and the treachery of one who was a friend. Tragically, this Stoic, who could sing the praises of everything that happened as the

---

20. Cf. H.H. Scullard, *From the Gracchi to Nero* (London: Methuen, 1976), pp. 245-46.

21. Julius Capitolinus, 'Marcus Antoninus the Philosopher', in *Lives of the Later Caesars*.

22. E.g., 2.3; 2.11; 4.34; 4.44; 5.8; 5.10; 7.41; 7.51; 7.57; 12.12.

gifts of a benevolent Providence, virtually cried out in his despair, 'My God, my God, why have you forsaken me?'

When Marcus became aware of the betrayal by his close associate, Cassius, he reportedly said to his army:

> Fellow soldiers, I stand before you to complain of my fate, not to demonstrate my anger. For what value is there in being angry at the gods who are all-powerful? Yet I must at least grieve for my undeserved misfortune. Is it not bad enough to fight in wars? And even worse to be involved in a civil war? And worse still is to discover that there is no loyalty among people (Dio, *Roman History* 72.24.1-2).

In Marcus Aurelius the problem of innocent suffering appears all the more frightening because an individual who trusted the gods to bring to pass what was good for the world was crushed by the injustice of his own circumstances. Despite the fatalistic optimism of *Meditations*, the emperor was 'totally unprepared' for, and 'extremely disturbed' by, the tragedies of life.[23]

4. *Biblical Characters*

a. *Literary*

While the character of Job could be considered to be 'historical',[24] the literary influence of Job as a book (independent of the protagonist's historicity) is significant. The story itself through the character of Job raises the question—as a specifically theological concern—why the innocent suffer.

The narrative is reasonably straightforward. Job is described as both the most wealthy and the most righteous individual of his time. He is God's servant.[25] The reader is told that Job 'feared God'(1.1, 8; 2.3) and this is rendered as *theosebēs* in the LXX and is regarded as a rare virtue.[26]

---

23. Anthony Birley, *Marcus Aurelius* (Toronto: Little, Brown and Co., 1966), p. 253. See also pp. 202-203, 252-57.

24. Or, depending on the definition used, 'legendary'.

25. 1.1, 3, 5, 8. 'My servant' is rendered as *paidos mou* in the LXX. Cf. the references to Jesus in Mt. 12.18; Acts 3.13, 26; 4.27, 30.

26. The term occurs in the LXX only in Job (1.1, 8; 2.3) and in Exod. 18.21. Cf., however, *4 Macc.* 17.15, see below, p. 67. For a New Testament example, see Jn 9.31.

The clear evidence of Job's piety and fear of God is most detailed with reference to his treatment of the poor, widows and the hungry. In defending his character, Job asserts that his benevolence was quite extensive (29.11-17; 31.13-23). Job might have cited Ps. 41.1, or a similar tradition, to justify his expectations that God would be gracious to him.[27] (Interestingly, the generosity of Job is a dominant theme in the pseudepigraphic *Testament of Job*.[28]) Consequently, Job regards himself as blameless, innocent and righteous. The term *dikaios* is consistently used to describe the protagonist's character (1.1; 9.15, 20; 10.15; 12.4) and Job would fully expect to be found 'not guilty' in any impartial trial.[29]

Through the intention of God, however, rather than being exempt from suffering because of his blamelessness, Job actually endures intense misery. Indeed, Job even regards God as a hostile enemy (6.4; 10.17; 13.24; 16.7-9, 11-14; 19.11-12). He is subjected to the loss of property, the deaths of his servants and his children, and painful sores on his skin (1.13-19; 2.7-8). Job becomes convinced that God is accountable for these tragedies and he gives expression to the bitterness of his soul (7.11; 10.1; 19.1; 27.2; cf. 3.20; 9.18; 21.25).

The issue of theodicy in Job is very complex but the simplistic view that suffering is always punishment for sin[30] is clearly rejected.[31] It is common to see Job as an example of the stern 'testing' of faith. Yet even if the character of Satan is regarded as the one who initiated the monstrous idea of evaluating the genuineness of Job's piety, God must bear the ultimate responsibility for Job's misery because (1) God endorsed Satan's proposal, and (2) Satan acted within the limits that God himself established.[32]

27. Thus, in the conventional theology of Job's so-called friends, when he suffers, he *must* be guilty of being uncharitable—22.5-11; cf. 24.2-14, 21.

28. Especially chs. 9–15.

29. Cf. Gerhard Von Rad, *Old Testament Theology* (2 vols.; New York: Harper and Row, 1962), I, p. 414.

30. This is the conventional theology of Job's friends: 4.6-7, 17-19; 8.3-6, 20; 11.1-6; 18.5-21; 20.4-29; 22.4-5.

31. God himself indicates that he is angry at the friends (42.7).

32. Among the questions that might be asked is why an omniscient God would need the results of such a test.

b. *Historical*
The subject of the suffering of Jesus of Nazareth will concern us in
Chapter 7, but it is important to introduce the broad outline of his life
and death even now. Within the biblical tradition, the most dramatic
illustration of innocent suffering is probably found in Mark's Gospel
where, as he dies tormented, the last words of Jesus are reported to be
'My God, my God, why have you forsaken me?' (Mk 15.34). The New
Testament generally, in virtually all streams of tradition, considers
Jesus as the innocent, righteous, Son of God who did not deserve to
die.[33] Perhaps it is not surprising that Luke chooses to omit Jesus' cry
of dereliction and adds instead as his last words a devout prayer:
'Father, into your hands I commit my spirit'.[34]

Generally it is accepted that Jesus consistently did good works and
deserved the favor and blessing of God. With tragic irony, the oppo-
nents of Christianity pointed to 'the abhorrent death' of Jesus as sufficient reason to reject 'the claims made by Christians on behalf of
Jesus'.[35] Even within the Christian understanding, the Resurrection of
Jesus is seen as overwhelming evidence of his *vindication, not forgive-
ness*, as one who lived a righteous life and did not receive justice in
being executed (cf. Rom. 1.4; Acts 3.13-15).

The righteous character of the life of Jesus is apparent (perhaps self-
evident) throughout the Gospels. He is confident even in standing
against the Hebrew Scripture in order to assert the will and intention of
God (Mt. 5.21-48; Mk 10.2-9). In the midst of his assurance, however,
Jesus demonstrates a childlike simplicity of faith which he demands of
his followers if they are to be in a proper relationship with God.[36]

The life of Jesus becomes a tragedy as the Gospels detail his rejection, humiliation, torture and crucifixion. Even though the so-called
'passion predictions' (Mk 8.31; 9.31; 10.33-34 and parallels) suggest

---

33. For example, 2 Cor. 5.21; Heb. 4.15; cf. Jn 8.46; Mk 1.11; 9.7; Lk. 23.4, 13-
14, 22, 47. See also William Horbury and Brian McNeil (eds.), *Suffering and Martyrdom in the New Testament* (Cambridge: Cambridge University Press, 1981),
p. 24.

34. 23.46. Cf. Roman Garrison, 'Last Words', in *idem, The Graeco-Roman
Context of Early Christian Literature* (Sheffield: Sheffield Academic Press, 1997),
pp. 48-57.

35. *Suffering and Martyrdom*, p. 166.

36. Mt. 11.25-27 = Lk. 10.21-22; Mk 10.15; cf. Joachim Jeremias, *New Testament Theology* (London: SCM Press, 1975), pp. 178-203.

that Jesus was aware of the 'fate' he would endure, the problem of innocent suffering nevertheless disturbs the reader.

Christian theology seeks to redeem the ugly execution of Jesus by claiming that his death was an atonement for, and a virtual purification of, the whole world (e.g. Jn 3.16; Rom. 5.6-10; Heb. 9.11-14). There still remains, however, the haunting question for all victims of undeserved suffering: My God, my God, why have you forsaken me?

Chapter 2

SARPEDON AND HECTOR: INNOCENT SUFFERING IN THE *ILIAD*

1. *Introduction*

The problem of innocent suffering continually haunts the traditions of the Greeks, the Romans and those of the biblical writers. The several attempts at theodicy have left many questions unanswered, and many agonies—physical, psychological and spiritual—remained to torment their victims without even the minimal comfort of a theological explanation. In considering the problem of how (and ultimately why) the righteous suffer, the logical starting-point in Greek literature is the *Iliad*,[1] believed to have been written by Homer. This is in all likelihood the most ancient, substantial evidence of Greek thought and provides a forceful and dramatic survey of a number of the themes that come to bear on Christianity's attempt to explain why the innocent suffer.

Homer[2] initially claims that all that happens, at least in the *Iliad*, is the fulfillment of the will, intention and foreordained purpose of Zeus (1.1-7). In fact, the petty indignation of Achilles is a central feature of the supreme god's long-term plan. This attitude is (perhaps inconsistently) maintained throughout the epic (cf. 19.90) and continues to represent a popular, contemporary 'theodicy': that whatever happens, the will of the god is fulfilled. The New Testament is often used to prooftext the inevitability of events in order to provide supposed comfort, particularly for those whose loved ones have died: 'For who can resist his will?' (cf. Rom. 9.19).

---

1.   Cf. Thomas Finan, 'The Myth of the Innocent Sufferer: Some Greek Paradigms', *Proceedings of the Irish Biblical Association* 9 (1985), pp. 121-35: 'For this question of the innocent sufferer in Greek literature I shall be concentrating on its presence at the very beginning of Greek literature—in Homer's *Iliad*'.

2.   Without entering into the authorship debate, I will use the name 'Homer' to refer to the final redactor of the *Iliad*.

While the *Iliad* presents a wide variety of characters and issues that warrant attention, one of the dominant themes in the Homeric epic that raises the problem of innocent suffering is the love that mortals and immortals alike have for their children. Parents, whether they are human or gods and goddesses, will instinctively seek at least to reduce or actually to eliminate the danger when their offspring are at risk. The well-being of the child (or children) often takes priority. This concern is an essential feature in the nature of every parent (cf. 9.323-24). It will provoke the question 'Why does Zeus forsake his own son?' and comes to lie in the background of early Christianity.

a. *Love of Children in the* Iliad
In the *Iliad*, a love for one's children is an important element of the story, which serves to promote empathy in the reader/hearer of the action. The work both begins and ends with strong testimony of a father's love for his child as the characters of Chryses (the priest of Apollo) and Priam demonstrate paternal anxiety and devotion for their respective offspring. Chryses seeks to have his daughter returned after she is taken cáptive by the Greek army, and Priam, leader of Troy, negotiates in order to recover his son Hector's corpse from the man (i.e. Achilles) who killed him.

Both of these fathers, who were enemies of the Greek army, are nevertheless portrayed as sorrowful characters who deserve the sympathy of not only the warriors to whom they appeal, but also of the reader/hearer of the epic.[3] It is assumed that a father is naturally concerned for the well-being of his children and strives to prevent their being harmed.[4] As this theme is repeatedly developed in the *Iliad*,

---

3.   1.11 introduces Chryses' concern for his daughter; Book 24 gives lengthy attention to Priam's desire to recover the corpse of his son, Hector. Finan notes that Priam is 'closely parallel to Job' ('The Myth', p. 128).

4.   E.g. 20.408-10. Cf. 9.481-82, 'as a father loves his only son' (cf. *Odyssey* 16.17-20; and 2.47; 2.234: 'gentle as a father'.) Zeus himself is a gentle Father in 8.38-40 (apparently repeated in 22.184; also cf. Epictetus, *Discourses* 3.18.5. See especially Abraham Malherbe's treatment of 1 Thess. 2.7 in ' "Gentle as a Nurse": The Cynic Background to 1 Thess. 2', in *idem*, *Paul and the Popular Philosophers* (Minneapolis: Fortress Press, 1989). Originally this was an essay in *NovT* 12 (1970), pp. 203-217. It is not Malherbe's concern to discuss the relevant textual evidence nor to focus on 1 Thess. 2.11, this text being of particular interest to us. Note the parental imagery in 8.271; 16.191-92; 17.132-35. Cf. Hector's action in 6.466-81.

Zeus' anguish for his own son, Sarpedon, is made more dramatic, but as well it becomes paradoxical: A father who is assumed to be all powerful approves (and, apparently, even plans), yet regrets, the death of his son.

In an early section of the *Iliad*, Homer briefly refers to certain brothers, 'the two sons of Merops, a man who was supremely gifted in prophecy and did not want his sons to go to war, the scourge of men. But they would not listen for the forces of Dark Death led them on.'[5] Merops, the prophetic father[6] whose love for his sons is to be trampled by fate, not only represents paternal compassion but is, if only indirectly, an eerie foreshadowing of the anxiety that Zeus too will experience in the death of his own son.

Even the immortals (as fathers and as mothers) are anxious to protect their progeny from the ravages of battle, and often seek to rescue their sons from dying in the war.[7] Significantly, however, at times the deathless ones do not act simply out of self-interest as parents. On occasion they intervene in order to preserve the life of an individual who, while special to them, is not actually the offspring of that god or goddess.[8]

b. *Alternative Fates*

In the *Iliad*, fate, as destined events in one's life, is sometimes described as less than predetermined. As the verb *amunein* is used of

5.   2.830-34 (apparently repeated at 11.328-34). LSJ regard this passage (and *Odyssey* 11.171) as referring to the goddess of Death. They also argue that the term *moira* alludes to the goddess of death in *Iliad* 18.119 (and *Odyssey* 11.292).

6.   Did he know that his sons would die?

7.   For example, Aphrodite's protection of Aeneas in 5.311-43; Ares' anxiety for Ascalaphus in 13.518-25; 15.110-18; Zeus' initial concern for the safety of Sarpedon in 5.660-62; 12.400-403; even as Zeus holds contempt for his son, Ares, nevertheless he is 'father-like' towards him in 5.895-99; Thetis's love for Achilles in 1.413-18; cf. 18.88-89. Poseidon is angry that his 'son', Amphimachus, is slain, 13.206-207. (Athene's protection of Menelaus is described as 'mother-like', 4.127-31.)A fascinating development of the *philon huion* theme is found in 24.118, 195, 333 as Hermes and Priam discover their close relationship, cf. 24.371, 373.

8.   For example, Aphrodite's concern for Paris in 3.373-82, 4.10-12; Apollo's early concern for Hector in 8.309-11; 20.443-50; (Aphrodite and Apollo protecting the corpse of Hector in 23.184-91, 24.18-21); Hephaestus saving Idaeus in 5.22-24; Poseidon's anxiety for Aeneas in 20.288-308. Cf. Achilles' comment about Aeneas in 20.347.

diverting or deflecting danger, shame or disaster,[9] it is often used of the immortals 'warding off' fate to prevent a warrior from dying or an army from being defeated.[10] Two passages which refer to Zeus' response to the needs of his son, Sarpedon, warrant specific attention as the tension becomes more intense. In 12.402-403 the *Iliad* acknowledges the saving power of the supreme god: 'but Zeus warded off the fates (*kepas amune*) from his child'. Yet later, in 16.521-22, when Sarpedon is in fact killed, the narrative reveals grief that such a noble warrior would die and the author comments, 'Zeus would not protect (*amunei*) his own child'. A more thorough consideration of the role and character of Sarpedon will be undertaken in a following section.

In a similar respect, there are a number of references to individuals escaping fate, often because of the intervention of the immortals, but sometimes these people are, apparently, simply 'lucky'.[11] While the death of Patroclus at the hands of Hector seems not only inevitable but actually willed by Zeus (15.64-67; 16.849), it is nevertheless claimed that Patroclus could have avoided dying on the battlefield had he heeded the advice of Achilles (16.684-91). Furthermore, the epic reports that Zeus seriously considered allowing Patroclus to live.[12] The ending of the *Iliad* would certainly be quite different if Patroclus had been protected rather than driven to his death by the gods or fortunate enough to escape fate.

The theme of alternative fates is perhaps implied when Zeus must weigh or measure the fates of the Greeks, the Trojans, Hector and Achilles.[13] If the results were absolutely determined (and known to the immortals), presumably the scales would not be needed. This idea of different potential destinies for an individual is especially evident in the case of Achilles who must choose between *dichthadias kēras*, namely

9. E.g. 1.396-400; 9.494-95; 11.277; 13.426; 14.369; 16.31-32, 74-75, 80-81, 512, 556; 17.507-11; 18.128-29; 22.84.

10. E.g. (cf. 1.67); 1.456; 4.11, 127-31; 5.9-24, 603, 662; 13.781-83; 15.372-76; 20.98, 122-24; 21.215.

11. E.g. 3.30-32, 360; 5.22-23 (cf. 5.311-17); 7.254; 11.360, 585; 13.566, 596, 648; 14.406-408, 462; 15.287-88.

12. 16.644-55. Zeus seems ready to reconsider the fate of Hector in 22.174-76. It is worth noting that both Patroclus and Hector are described as 'Zeus-loved' (6.318 [cf. 7.204-205]; 8.493; 10.49; 11.611; 13.674 etc.) This will be developed below.

13. 8.68-74 (*duo kēre tanēlegeos thanatoio*); 22.208-13 (*duo kēre tanēlegeos thanatoio*).

whether to die young as a courageous hero in the Trojan War or to live long in obscurity back at home in Greece.[14]

2. *Righteous Sufferers in the* Iliad

a. *Sarpedon*

The *Iliad* lays the foundation for consideration of the problem of the son of God as an innocent sufferer. While in many ways Hector and Sarpedon are virtually parallel characters yet there is at least one vital difference between them. On the one hand, Hector could only wish to be a son of God (13.824-25); Sarpedon, on the other hand, is in fact the son of Zeus. The *Iliad* reports that in contrast to the common metaphor of the universal fatherhood of the deity, Sarpedon was actually the begotten son of Zeus: The Olympian god had impregnated Laodameia and she in due course gave birth to Sarpedon.[15] Although this distinction between the two figures must be highlighted, still the similarities between them are significant and worth noting.

Both soldiers fight for the Trojans (Sarpedon as an ally of Troy) against the Greek army and both are valiant, heroic warriors (cf. 12.290-93). The two men are both married and have young sons (6.466-93; 5.478-80). When Hector and Sarpedon are killed, Zeus himself demonstrates concern for the care of their corpses (16.666-75; 24.74-76, 112-19, 133-37). Much more important, however, are the revealing coincidences that both Hector and Sarpedon are dearly loved by Zeus, the object of his compassionate pity, and that Zeus entertains the idea of changing fate in order to save them.[16]

The two also share a god-determined death. Hector is to be killed in battle by Achilles, and as Zeus allows events to move toward the fated slaying of his son, he regrets the approaching death of Sarpedon—to be killed by Patroclus. Hera, the wife of Zeus, intervenes,

> Are you seriously considering delivering yet again that mortal who has long been doomed by fate? Go ahead but know that we other gods do not agree. And another thing, so pay attention: if you spare Sarpedon to

14. 9.410-16. Cf. also 13.663-72 and the comment in Lucian, *The Patriot* 15. See also 20.336 and Lucian, *Zeus Catechized* 2.

15. 6.198-99. For a few of the references to Sarpedon as the son of Zeus, see 5.668-75; 16.459-61, 522.

16. Cf. Seth L. Schein, *The Mortal Hero* (Berkeley: University of California Press, 1984), pp. 61, 63. *Iliad* 16.431-38; 22.167-70; 24.66-70.

return home alive, be forewarned that some other god might also spare his son from the battle. After all, many gods have sons in this conflict...[17]

Zeus submissively allows fate to be accomplished but the bitter irony is that several of the gods and goddesses have indeed protected the lives of various individuals in the Trojan War. Rather than becoming angry or hostile, Zeus weeps: 'he showered tears of blood that drenched the earth, showers in praise of him, his own dear son, the man Patroclus was just about to kill'.[18] The son of God is slain and, in stark contrast to the literature of early Christianity, the supreme god (= Zeus) reveals his anxiety that his child suffered.[19]

b. *Hector*

Because of his resentment and anger toward Agamemnon and the lack of support from his comrades in battle, Achilles refuses to enter the conflict of the war when he is most needed by his fellow soldiers. His comrade, Patroclus, using Achilles' armor, hurriedly marches off in hope of rescuing the Greek army. Although he is initially victorious, Patroclus, the close friend of Achilles, is eventually killed by Hector, one of several sons of Priam and the greatest (along with Aeneas; cf. 2.816-18; 17.513) of the warriors defending the city of Troy. On several occasions Hector leads his troops in battle against the Greeks, and Agamemnon comments with apparent amazement, 'I have never seen nor heard from another that one man alone—and not the dear son of a goddess or god—could accomplish what Hector has this day'.[20] It is ironic that later when Poseidon seeks to inspire the Greek army to fight harder against the Trojans and Hector, the god charges Hector with arrogance, that he supposedly boasts that he is a son of Zeus (13.54; cf. Mt. 27.39-43). This accusation is probably understood to be false.[21]

Following the death of Patroclus, Achilles takes to the battle not to win glory for himself and so rid himself of the apparent shame heaped upon him by Agamemnon, but primarily because of his fierce desire to

17. 16.441-49, a significant echo of 4.28.

18. 16.459-61. Translation by Robert Fagles. For Plato, Zeus' anguish for Sarpedon and for Hector is scandalous, *Republic* 388c.

19. No early Christian text attempts explicitly to describe God's (presumed) anguish as Jesus dies.

20. A rather free translation of 10.47-50.

21. Cf. 13.824-25 but Priam may have encouraged such a belief, 24.258-59.

avenge the slaying of his dear friend. Achilles is consciously determined to kill Hector even though it will lead to his own early death.
While this seems, in many respects, to be the ultimate purpose of Zeus
and the foreordained destiny for the son of Priam, there are indications
that Zeus himself was prepared to question the justice of Hector's
dying.

3. *The Piety of Hector*

Throughout the *Iliad* piety, particularly in the form of sacrifice, war-
rants gratitude and blessing from the gods. Thus, at one point the Greek
army

> lifted their hands to the gods, each man crying out in prayer. Foremost
> was Nestor of Gerenia, who stretched his hands[22] toward the starry
> heaven. 'Father Zeus', he said, 'if ever in the fields of Argos one of us
> burned the fattened thighs of a bull or ram and asked you for a safe
> return and with a nod you promised, then remember it now. Ward from
> us, O Olympian, the day of doom. Prevent the Trojans from destroying
> us' (15.367-76).

This prayer was heard and answered. The practice of such sacrificial
piety was thought to warrant the favor of the immortals.[23] Inasmuch as
this form of worship often (though not always, 2.400-20) is successful
in that it serves to influence the propitiated god, it might be assumed
that if Hector showed abundant and conscientious piety through sacrifice he would thereby merit the continued protection of Zeus. In fact, on
two occasions, Zeus refers to Hector's sacrifices as apparently warranting a fate for him other than death at the hands of Achilles.

> Unbearable—a man I love, hunted round his own city walls and right
> before my eyes. My heart grieves for Hector. Hector who burned so
> many oxen in my honor, rich cuts...[24]

> ...the immortals loved Prince Hector dearly, best of all mortals born in
> Troy[25] ...so I loved him, at least: he never stinted with gifts to please my
> heart. Never once did my altar lack its share of victims, winecups tipped

---

22. For the idea that hands ought to be outstetched in prayer cf. 1 Tim. 2.8.
23. E.g. Piety and sacrifice are intended to appease Apollo in 1.(20-21), 64-67,
96-100, 147, 312-17, 472-74; cf. 8.238-44.
24. 22.168-70. Translation by Robert Fagles.
25. Troy was, in fact, Zeus' most honored city, 4.44-47.

and the deep, smoky savor. These, these are the gifts we claim—they are our rights.[26]

The piety of Hector, however, failed to save his life. Consequently, the *Iliad* confronts us not only with the question of the purpose of sacrifice, but also with the more disturbing puzzle concerning the horrible, fated death of a pious individual. With Lucian the reader of the *Iliad* might challenge Zeus:

> If this is so, that the Fates rule everything through what is decreed, why should mortals sacrifice to the gods, making huge offerings of cattle and praying for blessings from you? I fail to see what benefit is gained by this precaution when it is impossible through prayers to avoid evil or to receive a blessing from the gods (Lucian, *Zeus Catechized* 5).

4. *Hector as Zeus-loved*

The previously quoted passage from the *Iliad* refers to Hector's being loved (*philtatos*[27]) by the gods. A second reason for doubting the justice (and perhaps even the divine wisdom!) of Hector's death is that the son of Priam is consistently called 'Zeus-loved' (6.318; 8.493; 10.49; 13.674). It is to be expected that the reader/hearer would wonder, 'Why would the supreme god not protect the pious one he so loves?'

The death of Socrates, who was advanced in age, could be termed a 'god-loved fate'[28] inasmuch as he would be spared the many discomforts of one so elderly. It is at best ironic, however, and at worst contradictory, that Hector, a young man needed by his family and his community, and loved by Zeus himself, should be brutally killed in battle.[29]

Further significant evidence that the immortals genuinely care about Hector is found in his ability to escape fate in earlier circumstances (7.254; 11.360; 14.406-408; 15.287-88), Zeus' pity and sorrow for Hector (15.12; 22.167-76), and Aphrodite and Apollo's protection of his corpse (23.184-91; 24.18-21; cf. Acts 2.27, 31). This general theme

---

26. 24.66-70. Translation by Robert Fagles. Cf. also the answered prayer of a man loved by Apollo, 1.380-84.

27. For use of the term in connection with an affectionate desire to protect from harm, cf. 20.407-410.

28. Xenophon, *Apology* 32. See below, Chapter 4.

29. Making this mystery even more complex is that Patroclus (11.611) and the doomed Achilles (1.74; 18.203; 24.472) are also described as 'Zeus-loved'. That even those who are dearly loved by mortals sometimes must die, see 6.12-19.

of the 'god-loved' individual as a pious sufferer will have renewed significance in the biblical tradition.

5. *Conclusion*

Within the epic, which might be conceived as a tragedy, the love of children is a prevalent theme that provides a striking context for much of the action. The relatively minor motif of alternative fates provides a measure of hope that certain characters might continue to live and avoid death on the battlefield. This consideration then led to a discussion of two of the principal heroes in the story, Hector and Sarpedon.

Despite the traditional belief of religion, the *Iliad* frankly acknowledges that piety is not always rewarded with answered prayers, that even those who are deeply loved sometimes must die, and that those who are righteous, even if they be the children of a god, often suffer. The purpose of these apparent injustices, however, is not haphazard nor do events occur simply because of the whim of a god. They are in fact fated to happen.

Homer's apparent theodicy is grounded in the confidence that all that happens is willed by Zeus, even when fate seems to be cheated. This may be a philosophical impossibility; it may be a paradox. It certainly is peculiar theology. The *Iliad*, however, leaves the reader with the conviction of its beginning: The anger and subsequent wrath of Achilles, and all that resulted from them, ultimately were the will and purpose of Zeus. In the plan of the supreme god, these events were destined.

In this survey, I next turn to the figure of Heracles, a hero Homer describes as Zeus-loved as well as a son of the Olympian, who, according to tradition (in plays by Sophocles and Euripides), nevertheless suffers and dies as an innocent victim, tortured by the immortals.

Chapter 3

HERACLES: THE SON OF GOD

1. *Introduction*

The *Iliad* introduces two characters, Hector and Sarpedon, and through them challenges hearers and readers with the problem of why the innocent and the pious sometimes suffer and die, apparently forsaken by their gods. Heracles, while not an active character in the *Iliad* (or the *Odyssey*), nevertheless through Homer serves to raise the questions related to theodicy. When Achilles accepts that in killing Hector he will himself be doomed to die in battle, he expresses his decision in a comparison with Heracles: 'Not even the powerful Heracles escaped dying even though he was dear *(philtatos)* to Zeus... Fate and the terrible anger of Hera overcame him. So, if a similar fate has been established for me, shall I die' *(Iliad* 18.115-21). Much later when Odysseus visits Hades he encounters the ghostly shade of Heracles who moans, 'Though I was Zeus' son I had misery beyond measure' *(Odyssey* 11.620-21). Again the issue confronts the reader, why do the children of God and those who are dear to God suffer and often endure miserable deaths?

Remaining from the attention to the role of Sarpedon in the *Iliad* is the unresolved problem which emerges even more dramatically in considering the character of Heracles: why would Zeus allow or bring about the suffering and death of one of his innocent sons?[1] For a Christian theodicy the more significant parallel will be between Heracles and Jesus and the problem will become all the greater, primarily because in Christian thought Jesus is the *unique* or even the *only begotten* son of God. So Justin Martyr, while recognizing and affirming the numerous

---

1. The term 'allow' seems to imply a permissive will that simply chooses not to prevent an event from happening. While 'allow' does not prohibit the idea of *initiating*, it suggests that the 'allower' accepted the plan of another. The expression 'bring about' seems to imply causation and purpose. Cf. Jon D. Mikalson, 'Zeus the Father and Heracles the Son in Tragedy', *Transactions of the American Philological Association* 116 (1986), pp. 81-98 (89).

common features in the lives and deaths of both Jesus and the 'reputed sons of Zeus', goes on to argue for the *superiority* of Jesus (Justin Martyr, *First Apology* 21-22).

There are, in fact, remarkable similarities between the legend of Heracles and the Gospels' stories of Jesus, and there have been various attempts to demonstrate that the former 'has had a significant impact on the formulation' of the latter.[2] According to Aune, one of the more 'bizarre' theories was promoted by Friedrich Pfister.[3]

Pfister's hypothesis, that a Cynic–Stoic biography of Heracles was known to, and influenced, those who shaped the Gospel traditions,[4] while 'interesting' and a 'fruitful suggestion', has been rejected as claiming far too much.[5] While many of the 'parallels' Pfister refers to are intriguing, this argument is not of central concern for our purposes. It is of note, rather, that Pfister gives at least some attention to the contributions of Sophocles and Euripides to that Heracles legend.[6]

Pfister's failure to emphasize this development seems peculiar inasmuch as Hoistad, in his book *Cynic Hero and Cynic King*, has rightly observed, 'In Sophocles' *Trachiniae* and Euripides' *Heracles* the hero is a deeply tragic figure who meets his fate in the conflict between the divine and the human' and the protagonist is seen as a model for Cynics and Stoics.[7] Both of these plays develop the themes of innocent suffering and theodicy,[8] and they themselves offer numerous parallels with the traditions about the death of Jesus.[9]

---

2.   David E. Aune, 'Heracles and Christ' in David L. Balch, Everett Ferguson, and Wayne A. Meeks (eds.), *Greeks, Romans and Christians* (Minneapolis: Fortress Press, 1990), pp. 3-19 (11).

3.   Aune, 'Heracles and Christ', pp. 3-19 (11).

4.   Friedrich Pfister, 'Herakles und Christus', *ARW* 34 (1937), pp. 42-60.

5.   Along with Aune's essay, see Herbert Jennings Rose, 'Herakles and the Gospels', *HTR* 31 (1938), pp. 113-42. The quotations are from p. 113. Cf. also, Wilfred L. Knox, 'The "Divine Hero" Christology in the New Testament', *HTR* 41 (1948), pp. 229-49.

6.   They are rarely mentioned but see p. 53.

7.   Ragnar Hoistad, *Cynic Hero and Cynic King* (Lund: C.W.K. Gleerup, 1948), p. 24.

8.   Hoistad, *Cynic Hero*, pp. 25-27; cf. Mikalson, 'Zeus the Father', pp. 89, 91-97. Cf. also David Grene and Richmond Lattimore (eds.), *Euripides,* III (Chicago: University of Chicago Press, 1959), p. 267.

9.   Cf. Mikalson's description of Heracles of 'god-abandoned'! ('Zeus the Father', p. 96).

2. *Heracles*

This play by Euripides raises a number of sceptical questions about the supposed 'fatherly-goodness' of Zeus, who not only permits or endorses the slaughter of the sons and wife of Heracles, but allows (in apparent agreement with Hera) Heracles himself to become their maddened executioner.

Heracles begins with the anguished plea of Amphitryon[10] that the sons of Heracles might not die at the altar of Savior *(sōtēros)* Zeus[11] at the hands of Lycus, the tyrant-ruler of Thebes (*Heracles* 37-48). Technically this prayer is answered.[12] Thought to be dead, Heracles returns from Hades in time to put Lycus to death. Hera, however, then sends madness upon Heracles who slays Megara, his wife, and their three sons. Heracles faints from the madness and exhaustion. When he regains consciousness and becomes aware of the murders he has committed, he wishes to die, even to take his own life. His good friend, Theseus, convinces him to continue living and persuades Heracles to come to Athens with him.

While Theseus and Amphitryon demonstrate the loyalty and faithfulness of mortals, the alleged son of Zeus, Heracles, apparently has been forsaken by the god thought to be his father. The chorus mourns, 'Zeus, as though you had no offspring, madness...has trampled him down'[13] and 'O Zeus, why do you hate your own son this way, leading him to a sea of troubles?'[14]

a. *Love of Children in* Heracles

Threatened with death herself, Megara seeks to shield her children, like a mother bird protecting her chicks (71-72; cf. Mt. 23.37 = Lk. 13.34); her love for her sons is evident (e.g. 280). Amphitryon's love for his grandchildren and for Megara is also obvious in his confrontation with Lycus (170-235; 316-26; 339-47).

---

10. The mortal (step-) father of Heracles; the husband of Heracles' mother.

11. Thus, ultimately Zeus forsakes those who plead at his sanctuary! Cf. Epictetus 1.22.16.

12. The children are led by Heracles into his palace. They are killed by him there.

13. Depending on how this passage ought to be translated! 888-90.

14. 1086-87. Note the almost parallel 'leading' by Heracles of his sons, 631. Cf. the 'leading' of Jesus in Mt. 4.1; Lk. 4.1.

When Heracles returns from Hades and finds that the lives of Amphitryon, Megara, and his own sons are threatened by Lycus, he leads the children into the safety of the palace and comments on the universal love that parents feel for their offspring.

> For I do not fail to care for my sons. All mortals are equal in this—they love their children. The prosperous and those who are without differ in wealth. Some have; some do not. But they all love their children.[15]

The contrast between mortal compassion along with human concern for their children on the one hand, and, on the other hand, the silent disregard of Zeus for his son, Heracles, becomes a dominant theme in the play. The Olympian's lack of paternal love is revealed even in his unwillingness to rescue the sons of Heracles from danger. Amphitryon, recognizing his own helplessness, cries out to Zeus that, if possible, he at least would defend and save the children (cf. 43-59). Despite his piety, his prayers are unanswered[16] and he derisively addresses Zeus: 'Though I be mortal, I exceed you, a great god, in virtue for I have not abandoned Heracles' sons' (cf. 342-43).

b. *Heracles as Forsaken*

Amphitryon has already cast serious doubt on the expected 'fatherly-goodness' of Zeus.[17] In light of his own anguish it is understandable, but nevertheless dramatic, that Heracles himself, as the begotten son of the Olympian, rejects Zeus as being his father (1265). Heracles furthermore refuses to accept the mythology that portrays him as Zeus' offspring (1341-46).[18] The pronouncement of the chorus serves as a near repudiation of Zeus for his failure: 'It is just *(dikaia)* that a father defend his children' (583).[19]

Heracles comes to the frightening realization and its effect: 'The god does not care for me and I care not for the gods' (1243). In the midst of his suffering and his denial of Zeus's 'fatherly-goodness', Heracles considers committing suicide. Theseus, however, persuades him to continue living. While this is powerful testimony to the importance of

---

15. 632-36. Cf. Jesus' use of the theme to illustrate God's 'fatherly-goodness', Mt. 7.9-11=Lk. 11.11-13. Cf. also the song by Sting, *The Russians*.

16. Jon D. Mikalson, 'Unanswered Prayers in Greek Tragedy', *JHS* 109 (1989), pp. 81-98 (90).

17. Mikalson, 'Zeus the Father', p. 93.

18. Mikalson, 'Zeus the Father', p. 97.

19. cf. Amphitryon's accusation in 347.

friendship and individual perseverance, still Heracles has been forsaken by Zeus.

Innocent people have suffered; some have died. Zeus abandoned his guiltless[20] son to the madness sent by Hera. Virgil's anguished protest on behalf of Aeneas is appropriate here: 'How can such fierce resentment abide in the heart of a goddess?'[21] This abandonment by Zeus and Heracles' sense of being forsaken, the death, despair and misery forcefully raise the issue of innocent suffering. Euripides does not avoid the problem. It is as if he wishes to say that the mythological stories only aggravate, they do not solve, the questions related to theodicy.

3. *Trachiniae*

Sophocles' *Trachiniae* is the story of the suffering and coming death of Heracles. Initially the play introduces Deianira, the wife of Heracles, who is quite anxious about the hero, not only for his safety but even his whereabouts. Deianira is intending to send their son, Hyllus, to learn what he can about his father when she is informed that Heracles will soon return victorious from battle. He has sent before him a number of captives who win the sympathy of Deianira. One of those prisoners, Iole, a beautiful maiden, is particularly noticed and pitied by her.

Deianira is later told that Iole was in fact the cause of the fighting. Heracles wished to have the young woman for his bride and when Iole's father refused Heracles' request or wish, warfare was the inevitable result. Triumphant in the battle, Heracles intends to offer sacrifices of thanksgiving and Deianira decides to try to win back, through a magic potion used to anoint his sacrificial robe, the love and affection of Heracles. Using the potion that had been given to her by Nessus the centaur, a previous victim of Heracles, she fully believes that her husband's desire for her will be restored. Nessus's potion, however, is actually a poison that is taken into Heracles' skin, causing him tremendous suffering. Crushed and tormented by pain, Heracles asks that Hyllus help to put him to death by lighting his pyre. Hyllus is unwilling to actually set the fire but he agrees to help in every other way. Before his death, Heracles commands his son to marry Iole.[22]

---

20. Mikalson, 'Zeus the Father', p. 96.

21. *Aeneid* 1.8-11; cf. *Heracles* 1307-308: 'Who would pray to such a goddess?'

22. For a very informative introduction to this play, see P.E. Easterling, *Trachiniae* (Cambridge: Cambridge University Press, 1982), pp. 1-12.

a. *A Father and his Son*

Euripides gave particular attention to the theme of love of children as a
contrasting background for Zeus' forsaking of his son, Heracles.
Sophocles, on the other hand, stressed the dependence and loyalty in-
herent in the relationship between a son and his father (i.e. Hyllus and
Heracles), thus exposing the utter treachery of Zeus in abandoning his
son. This theme is worked out against the naive, supposedly rhetorical,
question posed by the Chorus: 'Whoever heard of Zeus unmindful of
his children?' (139-40)

This question is mockingly developed throughout the play and
reaches its climax in the final speech of Hyllus when the young man
says in disgust, 'The gods have no pity. They beget children and wish
to be called "Father"; yet they observe such suffering!' (1265-69). Hyllus has shown himself to be a loyal and loving son. In the midst of
Heracles' continual challenge that Hyllus prove himself to be his offspring (1064; 1157-58; 1178; 1200-201; 1204-205), the son continually
shows devotion to his father. Further, as much as piety would allow,
Hyllus would be obedient to Heracles, bringing a measure of joy to his
tormented, suffering father (1246).

When Hyllus first became aware that Heracles might be in danger, he
was anxious to leave home immediately in order to offer assistance to
his father (86-91). Furthermore, believing that Deianira had treach-
erously caused the later suffering and misery of Heracles, Hyllus curses
his mother even to the point of desiring her death (734-35; cf. 744-47).
To further demonstrate his filial loyalty to Heracles, in obedience to
him, Hyllus is willing to risk impiety, even patricide, in helping to bring
his father to the site of his eventual death (1212-15). Even more evidence for his submission to his father is Hyllus's willingness to heed
Heracles' request that the young man take Iole for his wife (1216-51).

As to a father's loyalty to his son, Heracles' conscientious attention
to his paternal responsibilities might be questioned by Deianira (31-33),
but he nevertheless made a detailed will to allocate property and make
provision for his wife and children in the event of his death (161-63).
The most significant indication of Heracles' trust in and faithfulness to
his son Hyllus is found in the giving of Iole to be the bride of the young
man. This is the climax in Hyllus's demonstration of obedience and it is
the pinnacle of Heracles' 'fatherly-goodness' to his son. The bestowal
of Iole must not be seen as a mere circumstance of the narrative or an
explanatory detail supplied by Sophocles to provide background to the

Heracles' legend; the event is 'organically related to the plot' and the objectives of the author.[23]

Heracles, minutes before his death, had no gift to offer his son. Nor was he able to reward the obedience of Hyllus with any treasure in his immediate possession. Aware that the young man, having lost both his parents, would be assuming the responsibilities and the opportunities of his new independence, Heracles gave to Hyllus the one prize he might still claim as his own, Iole. In his final act as the young man's father, Heracles demonstrated his intense love for his son and his deep sense of trust.

Through the behavior and deeds of Hyllus and Heracles, Sophocles illustrates how a father and son ought to interact and how their relationship can be based in an assurance of the other's loyalty and faithfulness. By contrast, Zeus' fatherhood and his abandonment of his son, Heracles, are shown to be brutal and, ironically, inhumane. The words of the play echo, 'The gods have no pity. They beget children and wish to be called "Father"; yet they observe such suffering' (1265-69).

b. *Heracles as Forsaken*

Although in the Heracles legend, Euripides,[24] and the *Iliad* (18.115-21), the goddess Hera is consistently blamed for the suffering and the death of Heracles, Sophocles appears deliberately to refrain from accusing her of being responsible for Heracles' misery in *Trachiniae*. In fact, concerning his suffering, Heracles himself says, 'This trial is worse than any sent by Zeus' wife' (1048-49). Rather, the harsh judgment of Sophocles is that Aphrodite/Eros is ultimately accountable for the torment of Heracles and that Zeus, both as the king of the gods and as Love's subject himself, is guilty as well (cf. 354-55; 368; 431-33; 443; 476-78; 488-89; 498-500; 514-16; 860-61). Indeed, it was sexual desire that motivated Heracles' lust for Iole and Deianira was prompted by jealousy to the foolish action, intending to recover her husband's affection, which led to the death of Heracles.[25]

---

23. James C. Hogan, *A Commentary on the Plays of Sophocles* (Carbondale: Southern Illinois University Press, 1991), p. 267.

24. Cf. *Heracles* 828-29; 855-59; 1127-28; 1263-64; 1311-12.

25. On Sophocles and his attitude toward sexual desire, see Roman Garrison, *The Graeco-Roman Context of Early Christian Literature* (Sheffield: Sheffield Academic Press, 1997), pp. 32-33.

The words of Hyllus (although this is uncertain) [26] at the conclusion
of *Trachiniae* are a virtual indictment of Zeus' responsibility: 'You've
seen dreadful dying and agony today and hideous suffering and nothing
is here, nothing, none of all of it, that is not Zeus'.[27] The piety of Heracles means nothing. Despite his offering sacrifice at the altar of Zeus,[28]
and his seemingly scrupulous religiosity, Heracles is forsaken by Zeus.
He who is considered to be the son of the god cries out, 'You, Zeus,
reward my worship with disaster' (993-95).

4. *Conclusion*

While the *Iliad*, through the characters of Hector and Sarpedon, generally confronts the problem that those who are god-loved, even those
who are a son of a god, sometimes are tortured and die as victims of
'Providence', the story of Heracles is more specifically a tragedy of
innocent suffering, again of an individual who is god-loved and who is
a son of Zeus. Euripides and Sophocles develop different themes in the
legend, but both present Heracles as loyal to his children and pious in
his relationship to his alleged father. Yet in both Heracles is destroyed
by the gods with the acquiescence of Zeus. Euripides and Sophocles
mock the mythology that fashions such a theology. As playwrights,
however, they raise the questions of theodicy without offering a
response that is more acceptable to philosophers.

Both Euripides and Sophocles regard Heracles as forsaken by Zeus
and question the justice of the Olympian's providence. Sophocles cyni-
cally provides his audience with the paradox of believing in the myths
and trying to understand the real world. The words of Lichas to
Deianira eerily echo, 'Do not have contempt for a message of Zeus'
apparent accomplishments' (250-51).[29]

26.   That Hyllus is the final speaker in the play, see C.K. Williams and Gregory
W. Dickerson (trans.), *Sophocles: Women of Trachis* (New York: Oxford University Press, 1978), pp. 93-94.
     27.   1276-78. Translated by Williams and Dickerson.
     28.   This seems to be stressed: 237-38; 287-90; 657-59; 752-63.
     29.   A loose translation.

Chapter 4

SOCRATES

In a fascinating description of a conversation among several of his friends, Cicero reports that he was a privileged witness to a philosophical discussion about the nature of the gods. One of those individuals present, disputing the concept of divine providence, echoes the common objection, 'If the gods truly cared for people, then those who are good would do well and those who are evil would be miserable, but this is not the case' (Cicero, *The Nature of the Gods* 3.79). In elaborating on this theme and explaining his own personal experience that confirmed such scepticism, the speaker comments, 'Why should I even mention Socrates? Whenever I read Plato's account of his death, I always weep' (Cicero, *The Nature of the Gods* 3.82).

1. *Introduction*

In contrast to Hector, Sarpedon and Heracles, who are for our purposes literary and perhaps even fictitious, characters, Socrates presents us with the theme of innocent suffering as an issue that confronts individuals in history as well as literature. Although it must be admitted that those who report the defense of Socrates at his trial surely have their own literary motives that shape what they write.

Socrates was a citizen of Athens in the fifth century BCE, a contemporary of Euripides, and it has been suggested that Socrates contributed to some of the playwright's works (cf. Diogenes Laertius 2.18). Socrates lived to the age of 70 years as a self-sufficient (but not materially wealthy) philosopher. The governing faction, however, regarded his lifestyle and/or teachings as warranting prosecution and he was charged with impiety and corrupting the youth of the city. Found guilty at his trial, Socrates was executed by being made to drink hemlock.

Plato and Xenophon, both of whom claimed Socrates as their teacher, are the principal sources for the legal *apologia* made by the philosopher, and they both argue in their writings that the accusations were not only unjust, they were actually absurd. Further, they both testify that an innocent man (perhaps even a perfect man[1]) was undeservedly put to death. Plato and Xenophon, while agreeing about the injustice of the state's ending of Socrates' life, nevertheless significantly differ in their separate portraits of their mutual subject[2] and whether or not his death was willed by the gods. For Plato, the death of Socrates was the result of the unjust actions of the Athenians; it was not the purpose of the gods. Xenophon, quite in contrast to Plato, regarded Socrates' death as a virtual mercy-killing by which the gods spared a man they loved[3] from the torments of old age. While Plato repudiated the suggestion that such a tragedy was the intention of Zeus, Xenophon argued that death rescued Socrates from the advancing ravages of old age. For Xenophon, the execution of Socrates was a 'god-loved fate'.

a. *Plato on the Death of Socrates*

Plato himself has an intriguing view of innocent suffering with an implicit theodicy that seemingly exempts the supreme god from the charge of causing or permitting evil. For him, the genuinely good person (perhaps the one becoming perfect), the one who is just and honest with others, ought to expect to be rejected, mocked, even hated by the majority of people.[4] This is stated as a general principle: 'the just person will be scourged, tortured, thrown into prison, blinded, humiliated, and eventually crucified' (Plato, *Republic* 361e-362a).

Plato seems to have regarded Socrates as a particular embodiment, if not a literal fulfilment, of the type of perfection that results in innocent suffering. In the well-known Allegory of the Cave, found in Plato's *Republic*, a prisoner chained in the darkness is set free (the reader, however, is not told how) and is able to come to the sunlight of truth outside the cave. The freed prisoner's eyes grow accustomed to the light and see

---

1.   Plato may have regarded Socrates as a perfected philosopher; see *Phaedrus* 246a-250c. Xenophon considered Socrates a perfect model of virtue; see *Memorabilia* 1.2.60-62; 4.8.11; *Apology* 5.

2.   An interesting parallel is found in the Gospels of the New Testament in their characterizations of Jesus. The Synoptics are similar in perspective to Xenophon's view of Socrates. The Fourth Gospel's portrait of Jesus is more 'Platonic'.

3.   To anticipate a later chapter, cf. Wis. 4.13-14.

4.   Thus the consistent theme in Plato that Socrates provoked the hatred and contempt of the people: *Apology* 21d; 21e (twice); 22e-23a; 23c; 24a; 28a.

Reality. Plato warns that if the one who has seen the truth returns to the cave, those others who remained in the darkness may become violent.

> What do you think would result if this person went back to the cave?...
> Wouldn't that person be regarded as a fool? The others would insist that
> the outside world was blinding and that such an ascent was not worth-
> while. And if anyone attempted to free them and lead them up, that per-
> son, if subdued, would be killed (*Republic* 516e-517a).

Plato apparently considered Socrates to be one of the prisoners who had been loosed from their bonds and come to the light. Tragically,[5] Socrates had gone back into the cave to try to set others free to see the world as it really is. Rejecting the opportunity to gain true liberty they instead murdered the philosopher.

Plato's view of good and evil is grounded in a virtually complete disgust with the ancient mythology. Much of Homer is censured for its potential to corrupt the young (*Republic* 377b, c; 378b-e; 379c-e; 381e; 387b; cf. Plato, *Euthyphro* 6a) and it is interesting to note that for this reason Plato protested against the suggestion that Zeus lamented the deaths of Hector and Sarpedon (*Republic* 388c).

For Plato, the god not only *is*, but *can solely be* the source of goodness and virtue. Suffering, disease and death[6] have a different (although not specifically named) source. Evil ought not be attributed to the god.

> For the god, who is good, cannot be responsible for all that happens as is
> commonly believed. Only a small part of life is god's responsibility, cer-
> tainly not the greater part. For we have a much smaller portion of good
> than of evil, and although the god ought to be regarded as the only cause
> of good, we must consider other causes of the evil (*Republic* 379c).

b. *Xenophon on the Death of Socrates*

In his version of the 'defense' of Socrates, Xenophon quotes the accused: 'Perhaps in kindness the god is on my side in securing the opportunity of ending my life at an appropriate time and in a way that is the easiest' (Xenophon, *Apology* 7). Xenophon apparently accepted this view and believed that Socrates met a god-loved fate (*theophilous*[7] *moiras*), escaping the miseries of old age and meeting 'the easiest type of death' (Xenophon, *Apology* 32; cf. *Apology* 6; *Memorabilia* 4.8.1).

---

5.   One might say 'Foolishly'.
6.   That God is not the author of death, cf. Wisdom of Solomon.
7.   Cf. Xenophon, *Memorabilia* 4.8.3.

Consequently, Xenophon needed no theodicy to account for the fact that a guiltless (perfect?) man, Socrates, was executed. While it was urgent to Xenophon to demonstrate the piety of his subject and to show that his death was unjust, Xenophon's *Apology* was not written in order to support a philosophical view of innocent suffering. Xenophon's purpose, rather, is to establish that Socrates in fact orchestrated his execution.

> Others have written concerning this and all have reported the loftiness of his speech, showing that this is how Socrates spoke. They have not shown, however, that he had come to see that death was more to be desired than life (Xenophon, *Apology* 1).

The 'loftiness' of Socrates' words was actually intended to prod the jury to come to a guilty verdict. According to Xenophon even this apparent arrogance seemed to have been planned by the gods inasmuch as Socrates was not inspired to present a successful (i.e. victorious) defense (Xenophon, *Apology* 1; 8-9; 22).

While Plato and Xenophon differ in a number of significant areas in their respective reports about the trial and *apologia* of Socrates,[8] they nevertheless corroborate each other in some of what they write. One of the principal features upon which they are in agreement is that the accusations against Socrates were both ridiculous and unjust. The trial itself was outrageous and a pious individual was wrongly executed for impiety.

There are two primary features of 'piety': (1) the belief in the existence of the gods; (2) the practice (often understood to be habitual) of religious or devotional action. Plato and Xenophon give emphasis to different traits of piety in their respective 'defenses' of Socrates.

2. *Plato on the Piety of Socrates*

While much of what each writes concerning the indictment against Socrates is substantiated by the other, Plato and Xenophon disagree about the meaning (and significance) of the term *impiety*.

---

8.   For example, on the issue of old age and Socrates' attitude toward living with the loss of some of youth's abilities, see Plato, *Republic* 328d-e; 329e; 331a. Cf. also *Timaeus* 81e. For other affirmations of the advantages of old age, see Cicero's essay, Seneca, *Epistles* 12.4-5, Musonius Rufus, 'What is the Best Viaticum for Old Age?'

Plato opposed the popular view of piety, namely that religious activity was by nature virtuous and pleasing to the gods. In the *Republic*, he mocks the common opinion.

> Whether in public or private matters, the unjust individual defeats any rivals and becomes wealthy so that friends are benefitted and enemies are harmed. Sacrifices and offerings to the gods are extravagant, service to the gods and to mortals surpass those of the just individual so that one could conclude that the gods care more for the unjust person. And many suppose, Socrates, that a better life is given to the unjust than to the just... If the gods not only exist but care about people, our only knowledge of them comes from tradition and the poets...who tell us that the gods are influenced by sacrifices, prayers, and offerings... If they are right then it is reasonable to first do wrong and then to use the profits to sacrifice. Doing right simply averts the wrath of the gods but brings no profit. Wrong-doing, however, brings profit and prayer may persuade the gods not to punish us.[9]

Not surprisingly, the ideal community would not allow anyone to say that the gods can be influenced with gifts (Plato, *Republic* 390e).

Consequently, Plato, in his *Apology*, gives virtually no attention to Socrates' practice of ritual or public demonstrations of religiosity. Instead he understands the accusation that Socrates was guilty of impiety as meaning primarily that he did not acknowledge or actively believe in the gods of the State (Plato, *Apology* 23d; 24b). This perhaps indicates that for Plato himself true piety is to be judged (by the gods themselves!) on the basis of an individual's convictions, not simply on the basis of religious behavior or habit.

The claim that Socrates was corrupting the youth is related to the primary accusation inasmuch as it was maintained that he taught young people not only to question and wonder but that he encouraged them not to accept the gods of the State (Plato, *Apology* 26b; cf. *Euthyphro* 3a-b). Meletus, the chief prosecutor, is portrayed as suggesting that Socrates' beliefs constitute atheism (Plato, *Apology* 26c, e; cf. 18c).

Socrates ridicules this proposition (Plato, *Apology* 27a-e) and asks whether Meletus may have made such an absurd statement because he simply had no genuine or authentic charge to try before the jury (Plato, *Apology* 27e). Although Socrates does not directly reply to this accusation, his defense is implicit in the numerous references he makes to 'the

---

9. Plato, *Republic* 362b-c; 365e-366a. Cf. *Euthyphro* 14a-15a where it is claimed that piety is absolutely not a gift or service to the gods.

god' (perhaps the god of Delphi, namely Apollo) throughout the *Apology* (e.g. Plato, *Apology* 19a; 20e; 21e; 22a; 23a-b; 29d; 30a; 33c; 35d).

Thus Plato regards the charge of impiety as an accusation that principally concerns the theological beliefs of Socrates and does not address his religious practice or devotional activity. In this light, the reported last words of Socrates ('Crito, we owe a cock to Asclepius. Do not neglect to pay it', Plato, *Phaedo* 118; cf. *Republic* 331b) may actually be a sarcastic comment by Plato intended to mock the ritualistic piety of the State.[10]

3. *Xenophon on the Piety of Socrates*

Xenophon, in significant contrast to Plato, seeks to defend not only the theological assumptions and convictions (*Memorabilia* 1.1.5) but also to assert the religiosity (and thus the public piety) of Socrates. As in Plato's *Apology*, the two accusations in Meletus' indictment are closely connected. In Xenophon Socrates replies, 'Tell the court whether you are aware of anyone I have so influenced that they have turned from piety to impiety' (Xenophon, *Apology* 19). In recalling and describing the character and habits of his subject as being virtually perfect, Xenophon asks with obvious scepticism, 'How could Socrates have led anyone into impiety?' (Xenophon, *Memorabilia* 1.2.2; cf. 4.3.18).

Throughout his work, Xenophon attempts to defend Socrates. He maintains that Socrates consistently, if only occasionally, demonstrated his personal piety both in his own home and at the altars of public temples (*Memorabilia* 1.1-2). Indeed, Xenophon strenuously argues that the piety of Socrates was identical with that of the State. If the Platonic last words of Socrates were widely known, surely Xenophon would have cited them in support of his claim.[11]

> To begin with his attitude toward the gods: both his actions and words were in obvious harmony with the Delphic response to such questions as 'What is my duty concerning sacrifice?' or concerning the so-called cult of ancestors. The answer was 'Follow the custom of the *poleos*'. That is the manner in which to be pious. And Socrates so encouraged others as well as himself to act piously. Any other course would be presumptuous and foolish (*Memorabilia* 1.3.1).

---

10. For a recent valuable article on these 'last words', see Glenn W. Most, 'A Cock for Asclepius', *CQ* 43 (1993), pp. 96-111.

11. In reply to Most, 'A Cock', pp. 97-98.

4. *Socrates as an Innocent Sufferer/Palamedes*

Plato and Xenophon agree in more than judging that Socrates was unfairly and unreasonably convicted and executed. Both report that before the jury, Socrates referred to Palamedes as another victim of a perversion of justice. In Plato's version, Socrates indicates that after dying he expects to encounter 'Palamedes and other ancient individuals who died unjustly' (Plato, *Apology* 41b). Xenophon's account of Socrates' words is more detailed.

> I am comforted by the case of Palamedes who died in circumstances like my own. And he provides us with a hero's song far more than Odysseus does. For he is the one who unjustly put Palamedes to death (Xenophon, *Apology* 26).

Further, this association of the two victims must have become somewhat common, for Lucian mockingly refers to Socrates as conversing with Palamedes in the land of the dead (Lucian, *Dialogues of the Dead* 417; *Menippus* 18; *A True Story* 2.17). The story of Palamedes was well known.

Palamedes is a legendary hero from the era leading up to the Trojan War. When Helen is taken away (or runs away) from Menelaus, her husband, and becomes the mistress of Paris, Palamedes is one of the first recruits to help raise a Greek army to recapture her and to punish Troy, Paris' home city. As Palamedes comes to Odysseus to enlist his aid and involvement in the military effort, Odysseus pretends to be insane with the apparent hope that his madness would excuse him from service. Palamedes realizes that Odysseus is faking his condition and exposes the masquerade. Grudgingly, Odysseus joins the expedition.

Odysseus, however, plots vengeance against Palamedes. Through treachery and deception and by planting false evidence, Odysseus succeeds in having Palamedes charged with treason. Unjustly condemned, Palamedes is executed (cf. Apollodorus, *Epitome* 3.7-8). The central point of comparison between Palamedes and Socrates is that both were innocent victims of injustice and were maliciously sentenced to die (cf. Lucian, *Slander* 28-29).

Plato and Xenophon disagree on several features of Socrates' *apologia* before the jury at his trial. Yet their reports corroborate each other in the particular evaluation that Socrates did not deserve to die and that the charges against him were outrageous. It is significant that both Plato and Xenophon write that Socrates at least alluded to the similarity between the case of Palamedes and his own: both individuals were convicted unjustly.

5. *Conclusion*

Hector, Sarpedon and Heracles dramatically present the problem of innocent suffering (and death) as a literary issue among the Greeks. The case of Socrates demonstrates that this concern is grounded in history: Sometimes real people are unjustly killed.

While several of the details of Socrates' life and teachings are scattered among the many records in antiquity, there are two extant, substantial sources that claim to report the *apologia* of Socrates when he was on trial for his life. These are written by Plato and Xenophon. Although these differ in a number of features, still they agree in describing Socrates as an innocent victim who did not deserve the sentence of death imposed by the jury. He is unfairly executed for supposed impiety and corrupting the youth of Athens. He shares company with the traditional Palamedes, another person put to death through injustice.

Plato seeks to avoid holding the supreme god responsible for the execution of Socrates. Instead he 'blames' the darkened, hateful, wickedness of the many that Socrates had tried to lead into freedom and light by means of the philosophical search for truth. Thus for Plato, Socrates is the model of the genuine lover-of-wisdom who suffers for his goodness.

Perhaps oblivious to the issue of theodicy, Xenophon nevertheless rescues the gods from responsibility for Socrates' death by drawing consistent attention to the likelihood that the immortals used the jury's verdict and the execution in order to spare Socrates from the inevitable decine of health in old age. For Xenophon, some good resulted from the injustice, and presumably the gods are deserving of gratitude.

Neither Plato nor Xenophon, however, provide a definitive answer to the problem. Why would the gods allow (or even plan!) an unjust verdict to lead to the death of a pious individual? History and its interpretation, like literature and its authors' perspectives, do not offer a self-evident theodicy.

Chapter 5

ROMAN STOICISM

1. *Introduction*

Socrates was certainly remembered as a victim of injustice, an innocent sufferer, and democracy was often dismissed as mob-rule because of the verdict at Socrates' trial.[1] Tradition echoed his name, however, not only in regard to his death, but also in praise of his virtuous life. He was regarded as a model worthy of imitation.[2] While several other people were thought to have lived in a manner that was noble or courageous, providing an example for many, it is significant that Origen, a knowledgeable Christian of the third century CE, draws particular attention to the character of Musonius (Rufus).[3] With considerable justification, Musonius has often been described as 'the Roman Socrates'.[4]

In the present chapter the focus is on the extant teachings of Musonius and two other of the Roman Stoics who believed that Socrates' life and instruction embodied many of the principles they professed. Using as background the example and words of Socrates (according to Xenophon and Plato), the developed ideas of three Roman Stoics, Musonius,

---

1. Cf. Plato, *Republic* 8.557-65; Aristotle, *Politics* 4.6; 5.5; Cicero, *On the Commonwealth* 1.42-47; 3.33-35; Seneca, *Epistulae Morales* 14.9; 104.28.

2. Xenophon, *Memorabilia* 4.8.11.

3. Origen, *Contra Celsum* 3.66. Abraham J. Malherbe observes, 'Musonius illustrates how philosophy was also thought to be effective in personal ethics', *Moral Exhortation: A Greco-Roman Sourcebook* (Philadelphia: Westminster Press, 1989), p. 31.

4. Cora E. Lutz, 'Musonius Rufus: "The Roman Socrates" ', *YCS* 10 (1947), pp. 3-147: 'The names of the Greek and the Roman philosophers are linked together as preeminent examples of men who professed the highest ethical standards and lived lives in harmony with their teachings' (p. 4). For a view on a separate issue (i.e. atheism), see W.H.C. Frend, *Martrydom and Persecution in the Early Church* (Garden City, NY: Doubleday, 1967), p 86: 'Rome had no Socrates.'

Epictetus and Seneca in their respective understandings of the purpose and value of suffering (or hardship) will be explored. Roman Stoicism provides the most significant non-Jewish, ethical parallel to early Christianity.

Socrates employed the metaphor of 'training' or 'education' in describing the necessity of preparing for the contest of life as a physical and an intellectual challenge. In this both the teachings and the lifestyle of Socrates seem to have provided the foundation for Musonius' own beliefs and priorities.[5] According to Xenophon, Socrates deliberately adopted an austere manner of living with the specific purpose of both training and strengthening himself to be self-controlled and consequently content in all circumstances. Socrates regarded the discipline of the body to be closely related to the discipline of the soul. He is quoted as saying, 'as those who fail to train the body are unable to perform those functions appropriate to the body, in the same way those who fail to train the soul are unable to perform those functions appropriate to the soul'.[6]

Thus Socrates was prepared to encounter and endure hunger, thirst, cold, heat and even sickness (Xenophon, *Memorabilia* 1.4.13; 2.1.6). This rigorous discipline of body and soul, producing self-control (the foundation of virtue, *Memorabilia* 1.5.4), enabled Socrates to accept all circumstances of his existence with a calm assurance; and, according to Plato, Socrates was in constant training for the athletic competition of life: 'I shall really endeavour both to live and, when death comes, to die as good a man as I possibly can be...and I invite you to share in this life and to enlist in this contest which I maintain excels all other contests'.[7] This metaphor and the call to exercise self-control are found in early Christian literature.[8]

---

5.   Musonius refers to Socrates' words or example in the texts Lutz calls 'That Women too Should Study Philosophy', 'That Kings also Should Study Philosophy', 'That Exile is not an Evil', 'Will the Philosopher Prosecute Anyone for Personal Injury?', 'Is Marriage a Handicap for the Pursuit of Philosophy?', 'On Food (B)'.

6.   Xenophon, *Memorabilia* 1.2.19. On training the soul, cf. Philo, *Virt.* 18.

7.   Plato, *Gorgias* 526d, e. For reference to the athlete's need of training, see Xenophon, *Memorabilia* 1.2.24.

8.   Cf. 1 Cor. 9.25; 1 Tim. 4.7b-8; Titus 2.11-12; Heb. 12.11; 1 Clem. 35.2; 38.2; 62.2; 2 Clem. 20.2, etc.

Roman Stoicism generally and Musonius Rufus in particular virtually echo Socrates' passion for self-control as the athletic-like reward of training the body and the soul for life.[9]

> We make use of the training common to body and soul when we discipline ourselves to cold, heat, thirst, hunger, not enough to eat, uncomfortable beds, avoidance of pleasure, and the patient endurance of suffering. By these and other exercises the body is strengthened and enabled to survive hardship, being rugged and prepared for any task. The soul is likewise strengthened, trained to be courageous through forbearance and self-control in the avoidance of pleasure.[10]

2. *Roman Stoicism*

a. *Musonius*

Musonius Rufus was probably born about 30 CE, but there is virtually no information available concerning his childhood or upbringing. It was as a philosopher that he accompanied Rubellius Plautus in exile in 62 and was himself banished to the island of Gyara by the emperor Nero from 65–67. At some point he taught a school of followers.[11] Very little other detail about his life and career is known.

Musonius maintains that when people, whether they are male or female, deliberately appropriate the tasks of philosophy they ought to take on the training and 'proper education' that would enable them to exercise self-control and courage in all possible circumstances.[12] While acknowledging distinctions in the abilities and aptitudes of the sexes, Musonius insists that the quality and content of genuine virtue is identical for both and that the practical (as opposed to the theoretical) application of philosophy is the means to a goal common for men and women.[13]

Musonius argues that this discipline and self-control should be developed and manifested in attitudes toward possessions, food, clothing and

---

9. Cf. Malherbe, *Moral Exhortation*, p. 31 which notes the parallel in Titus 2.11-12.

10. 'On Training' (Lutz, 'Musonius', pp. 54-55).

11. Lutz, 'Musonius', p. 45.

12. Musonius Rufus, 'That Women Too Should Study Philosophy'; 'Should Daughters Receive the Same Education as Sons?' (in Lutz, 'Musonius', pp. 38-49).

13. Musonius Rufus, 'Which is more Effective, Theory or Practice?' (in Lutz, 'Musonius', pp. 48-53). See also 'On Training' (Lutz, p. 52, lines 23-25).

housing as well as in matters of sexual conduct.[14] This thorough imple-
mentation of philosophy's training is to have a significant effect on a
person's response to hardship, even to one's own innocent suffering.

As a person seeks to develop virtue, it is natural, according to Musonius, for there to be difficulties. He insists that all goodness is acquired
through toil. [15] Claiming that it is worthwhile to bear in mind that hardships are sometimes endured for meagre rewards, he then illustrates his
contention:

> For we see acrobats unconcerned as they attempt their difficult routines,
> risking their lives in their performance. Whether somersaults over
> swords, walking high tightropes, or like birds flying through the air, one
> stumble can mean death. Yet these acrobats perform for small wages.
> Should we not be willing to face difficulties for the goal of perfect happi-
> ness? Certainly there is no other purpose in becoming good than to be
> happy and to enjoy a blessed life in all our days.[16]

Musonius, in the little of his teaching that can be recovered, apparently did not give much theological attention to the problem of undeserved suffering. Instead, he seems to have regarded hardships as an
inevitable feature of human existence which the individual who is wise
(i.e. the philosopher) would use to help exercise virtue and develop the
quality of self-control.[17] The immediate or long-range purpose of the
god(s) in human suffering or difficulties is virtually irrelevant to Musonius; the principal concern is how the philosopher reacts and whether or
not such rigorous experience is used to train, or properly educate, the
one who toils. Innocence is not significant; theodicy is not an issue.

Musonius rarely refers to the god(s) in any connection other than to
insist that human beings as moral agents are intended to reflect the
character of the divine. Suffering and torment on the part of mortals are
not considered to be problems threatening the goodness of the immor-

14. Musonius, 'On Sexual Indulgence' (Lutz, 'Musonius', pp. 84-89); 'On
Food' (Lutz, 'Musonius', pp. 112-21); 'On Clothing and Shelter' (Lutz, 'Muso-
nius', pp. 120-23'; 'On Furnishings' (Lutz, 'Musonius', pp. 124-27); Fragment 34
(Lutz, 'Musonius', pp. 134-35).

15. Musonius, 'That One Should Disdain Hardships' (Lutz, 'Musonius', pp. 56-
59).

16. Musonius, 'That One Should Disdain Hardships (Lutz, 'Musonius', pp. 58-
59).

17. Cf. especially Musonius, 'That One Should Disdain Hardships' (Lutz,
'Musonius', p. 58, lines 25-26).

tals. What is being tested is human virtue. It is Musonius's objective that individuals be inspired not only to submit to that test but to become stronger and more disciplined through it.

b. *Epictetus*
The pupil of Musonius who is most widely known and who may well have been 'the truest interpreter of the spirit and intent of his master's life and teaching' was Epictetus.[18] He was in many ways the most humble of the Roman Stoics at least from a social perspective, born to a slave woman and, in all probability, a slave himself. Born around 50 CE, Epictetus came to study under Musonius at some point in his life, and was banished by Domitian late in the first century. Settling in Nicopolis, Epictetus became a teacher himself.[19]

Like his master, Epictetus regards Socrates as a model worthy of imitation, not only as an innocent victim of a terrible injustice and yet unafraid of death, but in his life and teaching as a supreme example of Stoic values (*Discourses* 1.25.31; 2.6.25-26; 2.13.23-24; 2.18.22; 3.7.34). Indeed, the surviving words of Epictetus are even more dramatic than those of his teacher: 'Epictetus is not better than Socrates but it is sufficient for me not to be worse' (*Discourses* 1.2.36, cf. Lk. 6.40). He admonishes his students, 'though you may not be Socrates himself still you should live as one who wishes to be like him' (*Encheiridion* 51.3). He tells an Epicurean, 'Lead us to respect and even imitate you as Socrates brought people to respect and imitate him' (*Discourses* 3.7.34).

In emulating Socrates the disciple is promised a type of philosophical invincibility: 'Do any of you have this Socratic purpose? If you did, you could be glad even in illness or hunger or facing death'(*Discourses* 3.5.17-18). In this respect, a lack of self-control in any circumstances can become a dangerous vice.[20] Self-control, even in the act of eating, is pleasing to the gods (*Discourses* 1.13.1-2). Echoing Musonius's ideas, Epictetus regards self-control as evidence of a virtuous life.[21] The discipline of a lifestyle like that of Socrates will strengthen the

18. Lutz, 'Musonius', pp. 19-20.
19. W.A. Oldfather (ed.), *Epictetus* (2 vols; Cambridge, MA: Harvard University Press, 1967), I, pp. vii-xii.
20. Cf. Fragment 10 in Oldfather, *Epictetus*, pp. 454-55.
21. Fragment 4 in Oldfather, *Epictetus*, pp. 444-45. Cf. Lutz, 'Musonius', Fragment 38, pp. 134-37. Cf. also *Discourses* 2.21.9.

individual. Such exercise and training prepare the individual (like a true athlete (*Discourses* 2.18.27) for the Olympic competition of life (cf. *Encheiridion* 29; *Discourses* 3.25.2-3). Indeed, everyone has the potential to become 'perfect'.[22]

> It is hardships that bring out character. So when hardships occur, be aware that God, like a physical trainer, has matched you with a vigorous opponent. And why? In order that you might become an Olympic champion but such an effort requires sweat on your part (*Discourses* 1.24.1-2). Who then is invincible? The one who is undistracted by externals. It is like the case of an athlete. So one wins the initial round; what about the second? What if it be extremely hot? What about the Olympics? So in this case. The one undistracted by wealth or love, the one unafraid of the dark, unconcerned with glory, suffering, praise, or death. All these can be overcome. This one is the invincible athlete (*Discourses* 1.18.21-23; cf. 3.6.5-7; 3.22.102).

Within the context of this metaphoric terminology, Epictetus then regards Socrates himself as a champion at the Olympics of life, 'for his victory was over more than meagre boxers, pancratiasts, or gladiators' (*Discourses* 2.18.22).

The idea of providence, Zeus' governance and administration of the universe and all that happens, is foundational for Epictetus. He illustrates, more so than does Musonius, that theodicy is in fact a serious problem for the philosopher, not merely as an intellectual issue but even more as a personal concern. Fundamentally, Epictetus' view of life's difficulties is that God is 'training' or 'exercising' the individual in order to prepare that person for the athletic-like contest of everyday existence.[23] Consequently he argues that the noble individual will recognize that when difficulties are encountered, Zeus is 'exercising' (*gumnazei*) that person, and Epictetus ridicules those who cry out and object during such training (*Discourses* 3.22.56-57; cf. 3.20.9; 4.9.15).

Epictetus emphatically affirms a belief in providence.[24] Zeus oversees the world. People are to be the knowledgeable and appreciative spectators of the god's authority (*Discourses* 1.6.19-22; 1.1.7; 1.12.32-35; 1.4.31-32). His attitude is well-summarized in the words, 'Surely whatever pleases God is also what is best for you' (*Discourses* 2.7.13).

---

22. *Discourses* 2.11.9. This theme is seemingly echoed in the New Testament epistle to the Hebrews.

23. Thus the challenge in *Discourses* 3.21.2-3; 4.4.30-31. Cf. 3.24.112-14.

24. Among the many references, see 1.6; 3.22.4.

Thus, like Socrates, Epictetus is prepared for Zeus' signal that death is the appropriate choice (*Discourses* 1.29.29; cf. 1.9.16-17).

To resist the working of Zeus' providence is to fight against God (*Discourses* 3.24.24; cf. 4.1.101, 108-109; 1.12.25). Employing more appropriate military imagery, Epictetus repudiates those who protest the apparent injustice that afflicts the world: 'you fail to carry out the responsibilities assigned to you by the commanding officer, complaining when a difficult order is given, and you do not realize that you, as much as you are able, corrupt the army' (*Discourses* 3.24.32).

For Epictetus, the problem of innocent suffering is ultimately an issue of personal submission to the intention and purpose of Zeus, the Father in whom he trusts.[25] Consequently, Musonius' pupil is able to say, 'I consider the god's will superior to my own; ...my will is united with that of Zeus'.[26]

c. *Seneca*

Seneca was born in the Roman province of Spain around 4 BCE. He was educated in the capital of the Empire and became a lawyer, a senator, and, after a time of banishment, the tutor for the young Nero. Seneca's brother Novatus, or Gallio, is mentioned in the New Testament (Acts 18.11-17), and Seneca himself is sometimes thought to have known and been in correspondence with the Apostle Paul.[27] Tertullian, an early Christian and fierce opponent of so-called pagan philosophy, nevertheless regarded Seneca as a virtual Christian thinker—*saepe noster* (Tertullian, *De Anima* 20).

Seneca was not a traditional teacher of Stoicism in his own generation and culture. Like Musonius and Epictetus, he was insistent that personal conduct, rather than doctrine, made a person a true philosopher. Seneca has exerted particular influence upon later generations, however, through his several writings. He endured poor health, the isolation of his banishment, and eventually chose to end his own life when he was suspected of having participated in a plot on Nero's life and the emperor prepared to punish the apparent conspirators. As he died,

---

25. *Discourses* 1.3; 1.19.9; 3.24.2-3,15-16 (with reference to *Heracles*, 2.16.44; 3.26.31); cf. also 2.10.7; 3.2.4.

26. *Discourses* 4.7.20. Cf. Fragment 4 (Oldfather, *Epictetus*).

27. J.N. Sevenster, *Paul and Seneca* (Leiden: E.J. Brill, 1961); Robin Campbell (trans.), *Seneca: Letters from a Stoic* (Harmondsworth: Penguin Books, 1982), p. 24.

Seneca reportedly said to his friends: 'I do not show my gratitude in a will but I grant you my best and sole possession, namely, my pattern of life. Keep it in mind and your genuine friendship will know the reward of a virtuous reputation' (Tacitus, *Annals* 15).

Seneca did not simply recommend his own conduct as being worthy of imitation. Even citing the words of Epicurus to lend authority to the suggestion, he counseled others to adopt the revered figures of the past as role models (*Epistulae Morales* 11.8, 10; 52.7). While he often referred to the virtuous example of Cato, Seneca, like Musonius and Epictetus, cited Socrates as an individual who ought to be emulated. He believed that Plato and Aristotle had been influenced and shaped by the nobility of Socrates' way of living (*Epistulae Morales* 6.6) and encouraged those who read his letters to 'spend time with Socrates' (*Epistulae Morales* 104.21).

As Musonius and Epictetus use the athlete metaphor of the philosopher 'in training', so too Seneca regards fundamental self-control (*Epistulae Morales* 8.5; 13.1-3; *De Tranquillitate Animi* 9.2) as an essential element for the discipline that yields genuine happiness in all circumstances. In this respect, Socrates is likened to an invincible competitor (*Epistulae Morales* 104.27), and Seneca calls his readers to the goal of becoming invincible.[28]

> So many train their bodies and yet how few train their minds... If the body can be trained to endure the attack of opponents such that a person is able to last all day in the burning heat and dust, even while bleeding, then surely the mind is able to be trained to endure the onslaught of Fortune and to remain unconquered (*Epistulae Morales* 80.2-3).

This perspective shapes Seneca's view of providence. The genuine Stoic is able to find contentment in whatever happens by accepting all events as inevitable. The individual who is unwilling to suffer hardship is mocked: 'You are enrolled as a contestant in the Olympics but you

---

28. *Epistulae Morales* 9.19; 31.6; 71.22, 27. Early Christian literature made use of the athlete metaphor and the idea of 'training' to encourage commitment in pursuit of perfection/invincibility even where this might lead to martyrdom. See Lk. 6.40; 1 Cor. 9.25; Heb. 10.32; 12.11; 1 Tim. 4.7-8; *1 Clem.* 5.2; *2 Clem.* 7.1-6; 20.2, 4; Ignatius, *Polycarp* 1.3; 2.3; 3.1; Robert M. Grant, *The Apostolic Fathers*, IV (London: Thomas Nelson and Sons, 1966), p. 131; *Martyrdom of Polycarp* 18.3 (William R. Schoedel, *The Apostolic Fathers*, V [London: Thomas Nelson and Sons, 1967], p. 76).

have no opponent. You may gain the crown but you gain no victory.'[29] Suffering and difficulties are the 'challengers' who strengthen the athlete (*Providentia* 2.3-4).

If someone should ask about Fate, or Chance, or raise issues related to theodicy (cf. *Providentia* 1.1, 4; 2.1; 6.1), Seneca replies: 'Whether Fate constrains us or God orchestrates everything or Chance haphazardly tosses life, we must be philosophers. Philosophy is our defense. It prompts us to submit to God willingly or to obey Fortune but defiantly' (*Epistulae Morales* 16.4-5).

Like Epictetus, Seneca insists that he trusts the will of God even when it is manifested in hardship: 'When all seems difficult and laborious, I have trained myself not simply to obey God but even to agree with the divine will. I follow God not of necessity but because my soul wills it (*Epistulae Morales* 96.2).'

Seneca's attitude is firmly grounded in the conviction that God is a loving Father: 'God is our great parent, no mild instructor of virtue but educating us as a strict father would... God tests us, hardening us' (*Providentia* 1.5-6; cf. 4.11-12). This, expressed in language strikingly similar to the New Testament, is regarded as evidence of God's love (*Providentia* 4.7; cf. Heb. 12.6).

> Have you noticed that fathers and mothers demonstrate their love in different ways? A father insists that his children rise early to begin their activities. Even on holidays they may not sleep in. They sweat and sometimes they cry... God is father-like with good people...saying, 'Struggle with labor, suffering, and loss that you may gain true strength' (*Providentia* 2.5-6).

3. *Conclusion*

For Musonius, Epictetus and Seneca the issue of theodicy is to be considered in the context of discussing the idea of providence, that the supreme god oversees and plans all that happens. For these Roman Stoics, the question of the god's justice when the innocent suffer is seen as a dangerous expression of doubt concerning the ultimate goodness of Zeus in the limited perspective of human experience. The true philosopher's will and desire are submissive and yet somehow oblivious to cir-

---

29. *Providentia* 4.2. Cf. *Providentia* 3.3 where Seneca quotes Demetrius, ''No one is more unhappy than the one who has no adversity'. Such a person does not have the opportunity to be tested'.

cumstances. Hardship and difficulties are seen as mere training for the one who seeks to become invincible.

Socrates is the metaphorical Olympic champion who endured much throughout his life, trial and eventual execution, and he demonstrated a rigorous discipline in a consistent pattern of virtue. Thus he became a Stoic hero worthy of not only honor but imitation. Socrates' manner of living, and perhaps most noticeably his exercise of self-control as a foundation for virtue, merited recommendation from the Roman Stoics.

Such discipline in everyday conduct promoted a corresponding perspective on all life itself. Discouraging the act of complaining and the underlying dissatisfaction it reveals, Musonius, Epictetus and Seneca instead encourage an appreciation of all that the individual possesses and a willingness to trust providence regardless of one's circumstances.

Hardships and difficulties are understood to be god-given exercises intended to strengthen, even harden, the athlete-in-training, that is, the philosopher. This metaphor is adopted by the writers of the New Testament.[30] Paul is quite emphatic in describing Christians in the midst of adversity as 'more than conquerors' (Rom. 8.37); it suggests that those who suffer are like the Olympic champions of the Stoics.

Stoic resignation and acceptance need not be seen as surrender. Epictetus and Seneca emphasize an awareness of Zeus as father-like. Their submission to providence is not born of fatalism. Rather, it is an expression of personal trust in the loving purpose of the god.

While Homer's theodicy suggests that the gods are petty and random and Sophocles and Euripides seem to regard the gods as vindictive and unfaithful, Socrates and the Roman Stoics maintain that even in the turmoil and despair of suffering, god or the god(s) will be at work to bring about what is best. This optimism provides a virtual introduction to biblical theodicy as found in Wisdom of Solomon and the New Testament.

30. See Roman Garrison, 'Paul's Use of the Athlete Metaphor in 1 Corinthians 9' in *idem, The Graeco-Roman Context of Early Christian Literature* (Sheffield: Sheffield Academic Press, 1997), pp. 95-104.

Chapter 6

THE WISDOM OF SOLOMON

Within the history of the canonization of the New Testament as the establishment of a collection of 'God-inspired' literature, there are a number of intriguing processes that interweave with several developments in the experience and resulting theology of early Christianity. The Muratorian Canon is among the earliest extant documents which refer to a particular stage in the Church's attempt to authorize the 'scriptures' for its members.

This fragment, preserved in a Latin manuscript, dates from about 200 CE and is eighty-five lines in length. It is a virtual list of books, an 'anonymous catalogue' that introduces those writings which constitute the uniquely Christian scriptures of the scribe's community, which may actually have been the Christian community at Rome.[1]

The Muratorian Canon indicates that the book, The Wisdom of Solomon, was regarded as worthy to be included among the Christian writings which came to constitute the New Testament. That evaluation is noteworthy for a variety of reasons but is especially remarkable because The Wisdom of Solomon does not even mention the name of Jesus.[2] The inclusion of the book is in many respects mysterious and would have to have been rationalized by its apparent compatibility—in perspective and content—with the other works listed in the Canon. It is not my objective to pursue this fascinating issue beyond the suggestion that Wisdom's theodicy was considered to be 'Christian' (in some sense) and is, therefore, worth our brief attention.

1. Bruce M. Metzger, *The Canon of the New Testament* (Oxford: Clarendon Press, 1987), pp. 191-201.
2. Cf. Metzger's comment: 'Why this intertestamental book should be included in a list of Christian gospels and epistles is a puzzle that has never been satisfactorily solved' (*The Canon*, p. 198).

1. *Introduction*

The Wisdom of Solomon (from now on referred to simply as Wisdom) is an intertestamental writing that is normally associated with the books of the Hebrew canon or what is sometimes called the Christian Old Testament. Accepted as deutero-canonical by the Catholic tradition, Wisdom is regarded by Protestants as properly belonging to the Apocrypha, that is, those books that ought not be considered canonical. For our purposes David Winston's description is sufficient: 'The Wisdom of Solomon is an exhortatory discourse written in Greek by a learned and thoroughly hellenized Jew of Alexandria'.[3]

a. *The Perishable Body and the Immortal Soul*
Wisdom maintains that it was through the agency of the devil's envy[4] (which is never explained[5]) that death has come into the world. The wicked behavior of the ungodly has summoned death 'because they are worthy of his company' (1.16). A vital contrast is then established between the self-sacrificing lovers of wisdom and life (the righteous) and the hedonistic death-lovers (the unrighteous). As the latter are 'friends of death' and deserving of its companionship, so the former are described as 'friends of God',[6] worthy of him (3.5; cf. 6.16).

While Wisdom affirms that all things have the imperishable (*aphtharton*) spirit of God within them (12.1) and that human beings were made in the image of God, intended to be 'uncorrupted' (*ep'aphtharsia*) (2.23), the tragic and undeniable reality of death is acknowledged. Even so, death is regarded as somehow independent of God's original creative purpose. Implicitly, then, Wisdom claims that creation has 'fallen'. The author insists: 'Death was not made by God nor is God delighted when those who are living die' (1.13). Consequently, the existence of death is potentially the cause of significant theological

3.   David Winston, *The Wisdom of Solomon* (Garden City, NY: Doubleday, 1979), p. xi.
4.   2.24. Wisdom nowhere else refers to the *diabolos*. In an interesting parallel, which will be explored in the next chapter, Heb. 2.14 is the only occurence of *diabolos* in the entire letter/epistle.
5.   Cf. Theophilus, *Ad Autolycum* ch. 19; see also *1 Clem.* 3.4.
6.   7.14, 27. For Epictetus as a friend of God, see *Discourses* 4.3.9; cf 2.16.44. See also Philo, *Omn. Prob. Lib.* 42.

problems (including theodicy) for the author.[7] Imperishability apparently becomes attainable only through wisdom (6.17-20) and this is usually described in the book as immortality, the overcoming of death.

The unrighteous often take that which truly is perishable (*phthartos*) and make it into a god to be worshiped by idolators. Such a corruption is an abomination; God's creation is misused and people's souls stumble (14.8-11; cf. 13.18). In this context it would seem that Wisdom allows for the view that souls pre-exist their incarnation as human beings.[8] The author maintains that because he (or his soul) was 'good', he entered a pure body[9] and that a perishable (*phthartos*) body is a burden to the soul.[10] In one of Wisdom's discussions of idolatry he refers to death as a time to return our 'souls which are out on loan' (15.8; cf. Lk. 12.20).

b. *The Death of the Righteous*
When the righteous (namely those who do not worship idols but instead honor and serve the Creator of the universe) shed their bodies, the earthy tent (9.15; cf. 2 Cor. 5.1-4) (thus conquering death), then their souls are free to appropriate fully the immortality they have long anticipated. For according to Wisdom, 'righteousness is deathless' (*athanatos*, 1.15).

While, on the one hand, this hope enables Wisdom to postpone divine justice until eternity and so uphold God's *ultimate* righteousness, the author is still confronted, on the other hand, with an important theological difficulty. If it is admitted that righteous people inevitably fall victim to mortality (cf. 18.20), and if it is maintained that God, while all-powerful, sanctions and at least permits these deaths, how can it be argued that the perishability of the body was not divinely intended? Further, the deaths of some righteous individuals at a young age would aggravate this concern.

The book of Proverbs might have been appealed to in support of the idealistic claim that at least the wise and righteous could be expected to

---

7.   The title of Michael Kolarcik's work is intriguing: *The Ambiguity of Death in the Book of Wisdom 1–6* (Rome: Pontifical Biblical Institute, 1991). The Gospel of John reflects a similar (though quite different) problem; see 8.51-53.

8.   Cf. Winston, *Wisdom*, pp. 25-32.

9.   8.20. A comparison to Heb. 10.5 seems inevitable.

10.   9.15. Cf. Epictetus in Fragment 26 (Oldfather, *Epictetus*)/Marcus Aurelius, *Meditations* 4.41.

live many years, to enjoy a prolonged life (Prov. 3.16; 10.27; cf. also Sir. 1.12, 20). Wisdom, however, confronts the often harsh truth that not only do the righteous eventually die, but sometimes they have early or premature, deaths (cf. 4.7). The author nevertheless finds in the experience of the ancient Enoch (who did not die!) (Gen. 5.18-24) a model or type for the righteous who 'depart' early: 'There was one who pleased God[11] and was loved by God. While living among sinners, he was snatched up (cf. Gen. 5.24; Heb. 11.5). He was caught up so that evil would not alter his understanding or treachery corrupt his soul' (4.10-11).

Wisdom not only regards the early deaths of the righteous to be similar to the experience of Enoch but further considers these 'departures' evidence that those who have died, in some way, have been 'perfected' (*teleiōtheis...telestheisa*).[12] However, if the unrighteous should die young, the author is insistent that this ought not be seen as an indication that God is pleased with the conduct of their lives (3.18).

Whether brief or long, the existence and behavior of the righteous individual are characterized as victorious in the athletic-like contest of life where the achievement of virtue is the prize. Although there is no mention of *Olympic*-style competition and training, the common metaphor of the champion at the games is employed by the author to illustrate the benefits of a righteous life guided by wisdom.[13] As Enoch is the model for the godly who depart (from life) early, the patriarch Jacob is regarded as the example of the one who wrestles with obstacles and prevails: '...in his strenuous contest Wisdom gave him the victory in order that he might realize that piety is more powerful than all else' (10.12).

Wisdom leads to a virtuous life, one that is honored both in memory and by imitation, so that throughout time, 'it proceeds wearing a crown, a victor in the contest for prizes that are pure' (4.2). Wisdom, through virtue, bestows the four Platonic/Stoic qualities of self-control,

---

11. For the theme of pleasing God, see 4.14; 9.9, 10, 18.

12. 4.13, 16. Is there any relationship between Wisdom's view of 'perfection' and that found in Heb. (2.10; 5.9; 7.28, etc.)? Heb. 12.23 may certainly be an echo of Wisdom's view. Other texts that may bear on this discussion include Eusebius, *Hist. Eccles.* 3.35; 7.15; Cicero, *Tusc* 1.45; 5.5.

13. As we have seen, the Roman Stoics made frequent use of this imagery.

prudence, justice and courage[14] upon those who 'love righteousness' (8.7; cf. 1.1; Heb. 1.9).

Clearly, this is an indication that Wisdom emerged in a generally Hellenistic (as opposed to a restricted Palestinian) environment. A significant parallel of this athlete metaphor is found in *4 Maccabees*.

> Surely the contest in which they participated was divine for at that time virtue came to test their endurace; the prize for the victor was im-mortality in endless living. Eleazar was the first to enter the contest, the mother of the seven sons next came in, and the brother themselves contended. The tyrant was the opponent. The world and all those living were witnesses. Fear of God[15] won the victory and gave the crown to its own athletes. Who was not amazed at these athletes of the divine decree? Who was not astounded? (*4 Macc.* 17.11-16; cf. 6.10; 11.20. Cf. Philo, *Omn. Prob. Lib.* 26).

2. *The Reward of Righteousness*

a. *The Righteous as God's Children*

Wisdom exhibits awareness that parents ought to love and protect their children. While the supposed expression of grief is condemned, the author assumes that among the pagans too a father would mourn the death of his child (14.15). Within Judaism, it is maintained that Abraham was strengthened and sustained by spiritual wisdom because of his 'compassion for his child' (10.5). Although Wisdom does not explicitly draw the contrast, still the unrighteous are portrayed as abusive towards their own offspring.[16] It is certainly implied that the Canaanites were defeated by God both because of their abominable practice of child-sacrifice and in order that Israel might settle in the Promised Land and establish a 'worthy colony' of God's children.[17] This claim is similar to the later assertion that the Egyptians' grief over the deaths of their

---

14. E.g., Plato, *Phaedo* 69c; Winston (*Wisdom*, p. 194) refers to Zeno's views found in H. von Arnim (ed.), *Stoicorum Veterum Fragmenta* (Stuttgart, 1964), III, pp. 255-61.

15. *theosebeia.*

16. 12.5-6; 14.23. Cf. 11.7. There is a bitter irony in the fact that Abraham's willingness to slay Isaac as an offering to the Lord is regarded as a heroic act of faith while the child-sacrifices of 'unrighteous' peoples is considered murderous.

17. 12.5-7. While the term *pais* is often ambiguous in meaning, here it is made clear by the context.

firstborn children in the Passover was the spark that ennabled them to
recognize Israel as God's son.[18]

Wisdom consistently regards the righteous people of the nation as the
sons and daughters, or collectively the child, of God.[19] In a strong
affirmation of God's providential power and supervision, the author of
Wisdom addresses God in prayer, 'O Father…'[20] Such a conviction,
however, also entangles Wisdom in the problem of innocent suffering:
if God is the Father of the righteous and if fathers are concerned for the
well-being of their children, and if God is all-powerful and in control of
all things, then why do the righteous often suffer at the hands of the
unrighteous?

b. *God's Fatherly Testing of the Righteous*
Insisting that God is the (heavenly) Father of righteous Israelites, Wisdom confronts the issue of why some innocent Jews have nevertheless
been tormented and experienced obstacles. The resolution of this difficulty is found in the claim that God, like a father, tests (*epeirasthēsan*)
his children as a type of admonishment or discipline.[21] This testing is
often carried out through the oppression of the righteous by those who
are considered foolish, blinded by mortality.

> [the unrighteous say to themselves] 'Let us ambush the righteous one…
> who claims knowledge of God and status as a child of the Lord (cf. *Iliad*
> 13.54). supposing the end of the righteous to be happy, claiming God as
> Father. Let us evaluate the truth of such words, testing [*peirasomen*] the
> end of this person's life. For if the righteous one is indeed a child of
> God, God will provide help… Let us find out through insults and tor-
> ture… Let us condemn the righteous one to a death without honor' (2.12-
> 20).

There are two apparent streams of tradition shaping the theodicy of
Wisdom. The suffering of the righteous is interpreted from the Jewish
perspective of 'divine testing' and 'discipline' and from the Hellenistic

---

18.   18.12-13. It is possible, however, to find in Wisdom evidence that even the
unrighteous are God's children (12.25).

19.   2.13, 17-18; 5.5; 9.7; 11.10; 12.7, 19-21; 14.3; 16.10, 21, 26; 18.4; 19.6;
20.6.

20.   14.3. For other passages referring to God's omnipotence or omniscience, see
11.17 (*pantodunamos*); 11.20-21, 23; 12.12, 18; 15.1; 16.15, etc.

21.   11.9-10; see 16.6; cf. Deut. 8.5; 1 Cor. 4.14. The author of Wisdom would
likely add, 'Woe to those who do not heed such admonishing' (cf. 12.26).

understanding of hardship as a type of athletic training for the soul.

One of the earliest events[22] which became foundational for Israel's faith was the willingness of Abraham to 'sacrifice' (i.e. kill) his son Isaac as an offering to the Lord. This episode is often, as in Gen. 22.1, described as God's *test* of Abraham (cf. esp. Heb. 11.17-19). The idea of a divine test is rather prominent in Deuteronomy (8.2; 13.3; 33.8) and Sirach suggests that wisdom herself (personified) severely tests those who attempt to follow her (4.17).

Thus, the theme of suffering or hardship as God's 'discipline' also has definite roots in Judaism (Deut. 4.36; cf. 32.10; Sir. 6.32; 18.13-14). Significantly, the idea of properly raising a child underlies the interpretation of and leads naturally to the view that the children of God receive God's discipline.

> The one who withholds the rod, hates the son, but the one who loves him is diligent to discipline him (Prov. 13.24).

> The one who loves a son will chastise him often in order that the way he turns out is pleasing. The one who disciplines a son will find it profitable...(Sir. 30.1-2a)

> The LORD disciplines the one he loves, as a father the son with whom he is pleased (Prov. 3.12; cf. Philo, *De Congressu Quaerendae Eruditionis Studies* 177).

> In your heart know that as a man disciplines his son, so your God, the LORD, disciplines you (Deut. 8.5).

With the confidence that the persecuted and suffering righteous ones (i.e. those who love wisdom) are God's children, Wisdom's theodicy is well-summarized in 3.5: 'Disciplined a little, they will receive tremendous blessing because God tested them and found them worthy of himself'. The next chapter will seek to demonstrate that this theme of 'divine discipline' is especially prominent as the New Testament document, Hebrews, attempts to understand the purpose of God in the suffering of innocent people. Although the metaphor of athletic competition and training is evident, it is the interpretation suggested by the Scripture which most influenced the author of Hebrews.

Wisdom also finds hope in the ultimate justice of God in the doctrine of Judgment Day. As Wisdom acknowledges, often good people die miserable deaths. Sometimes they die at a young age. Yet, as noted in a

---

22. Whether historical or legendary.

previous section, Wisdom is not troubled by the apparent injustice: 'Even if the righteous have an early death, still they will be at rest'.[23] Despite the severe chastening of God's children, Wisdom foresees an immortality of divine mercy awaiting them (12.21-22). Indeed, it is maintained that the faithful will be with God 'in love' (3.9) because Wisdom offers the assurance that 'the righteous are immortal, rewarded by the Lord. The Most High takes care of them' (5.15).

c. *Justice in the Afterlife*

The author of Wisdom is well aware of the injustice of the visible world, the suffering of the righteous at the hands of the unrighteous, and the premature death of many godly individuals. Wisdom, at the same time, affirms a belief in the over-riding will of God. Nothing—not even death—is outside of the present purpose (and power) of God.

For Wisdom, these two convictions must be reconciled in a theodicy that recognizes the ultimate justice of God. The author expresses assurance that on the Judgment Day to come evil will be severely punished and virtue will be rewarded. 'The ungodly will come with dread as their sins are tallied and their lawlessness will convict them. The godly will stand in tremendous confidence even among those who have oppressed them' (4.20–5.1).

At the final accounting in the invisible world, God's justice will be established. The righteous, despite their once apparent rejection, shall receive the blessing of immortality for their pure souls (2.22; 3.4) and the unrighteous, who have long been observed by God, will surely be punished, perhaps destroyed (1.6, 8, 11; 5.17-23).[24]

Wisdom, then, maintains that although the righteous are the children of God, they are tested by God and allowed to suffer in the present age. Death may seem tragic but it is occasionally the means God has chosen to rescue the righteous from the misery of the mortal or perishable condition of human life. The unrighteous are given the opportunity to enjoy existence but they misuse God's creation and seek to harm the elect. For Wisdom, this ugly injustice will be corrected on the day of judgment.

---

23. 4.7. For a striking parallel for many of these themes, see Plutarch, *Consolation ad Apollonium* 117D: 'Perhaps God, in a fatherly concern for humanity, and seeing the future, removes some people from life prematurely'.

24. Wisdom does not have a concept of 'hell'.

d. *Conclusion*

Earlier it was suggested that the Wisdom of Solomon was included in the Muratorian Canon's list of writings appropriate to a Christian collection of writings primarily because the book was thought to be compatible with the standards and beliefs of the primitive Church. Surely the seeming prophecy of Wis. 2.12-20 (cf. Mt. 27.39-43), although making part of Wisdom acceptable, even God-inspired, would only promote the inclusion of the book among the writings of the Prophets in the Hebrew canon.

That Wisdom is embraced in the Muratorian Canon as a *Christian* writing at least suggests the theory that certain ideas, themes or doctrines in the book were thought to complement or substantiate those teachings found in the literature of early Christianity.

Such a possibility seems plausible in light of the following: (1) A consistent distinction is made between the righteous and the unrighteous but with a theodicy that maintains that both the benefits and the difficulties of life are given by God to those who are godly as well as to those who are not (cf. Mt. 5.45). Furthermore, the hardships of the righteous are regarded as a means by which the children of God are 'tested';[25] (2) While Wisdom does not advocate a belief in resurrection of the body, its view of the soul's immortality is consistent with some early Christian theology (cf. 2 Cor. 5.4-5; even 1 Cor. 15.51-55); (3) The frequent suffering of God's children (i.e. the righteous) is an indication of participation in the 'fallenness' of creation which God will redeem from its bondage to mortality (cf. Rom. 8.14-25).

Wisdom of Solomon is an important transition from the theodicy of hellenistic Judaism to certain views held within early Christianity. Through the process of canonization, the latter has become a position sanctioned by the authority of the Bible.

---

25. Cf. 'lead us not to the time of testing', Mt. 6.13 = Lk. 11.4. See especially the following chapter of the present work.

Chapter 7

EARLY CHRISTIAN LITERATURE

This chapter will give significant attention to the figures of Jesus as an innocent sufferer and (from the perspective of the letter to the Hebrews) to the individual Christian as a child of God, who in spite of that loving relationship must often endure hardship or even violence. At the same time, however, the purpose of the present study is to begin drawing together certain common features of the Greek, Roman and biblical traditions concerning righteous (or pious) men and women who are apparently god-forsaken in their misery.

As the analysis of the *Iliad* began with a consideration of the theme 'Love of Children', so it is appropriate in this chapter to pursue that subject within the New Testament context. Other issues or topics that helped to illumine the implicit theodocies of Euripides, Sophocles, Plato, Xenophon, the Roman Stoics, or the author of Wisdom of Solomon will be re-examined from a New Testament perspective. These include 'Jesus as God's Beloved Son', comparing the deaths of Jesus and Sarpedon; and 'God's Fatherly Testing', exploring the concept of testing as a means of explaining or rationalizing the suffering of the innocent.

This survey and analysis are intended to demonstrate the universality of several of the themes found in the Greek, Roman and biblical traditions that raise questions of theodicy and to attempt, if in only a meager way, to articulate answers.

1. *Introduction*

...the children should not provide for the parents; rather, the parents ought to set aside for their children...[1]

1. 2 Cor. 12.14. For the general theme of parental responsibility, cf. Hermas *Vision* 1.3.1-2; 2.3.1; 3.1.6.

a. *Love of Children in the Gospel Tradition*
It is not our objective, certainly not our responsibility, to wrestle with the questions that bear directly on the historical accuracy of the Gospels' accounts nor to determine the literary relationships which underlie the Synoptic Problem. There is not a need to explore the probability that a particular tradition[2] or Evangelist's source may or may not echo a specific 'happening' with roots in history, in the life and ministry of Jesus, the so-called *Sitz im Leben Jesu*. It is enough to recognize the Evangelists' interest in presenting these traditions (i.e. the ones they have selected) to their readers.

The canonical Gospels give prominence to the love that a parent has for a child. There is a clear demonstration of the passionate desire for the well-being, the prestige, the health, even the life of one's offspring and this provides the justification for early Christianity's parabolic claim that God, like a father, loves all people who are the children of God. Matthew and Luke both preserve the logion of Jesus that affirms the natural (if imperfect) impulse of parents to provide for their children and then uses that 'truth' to express an insight about the character of God: 'Would any of you give his son a stone when asked for bread, or a snake when asked for a fish? If you who are evil know to give good gifts to your children, how much more will your heavenly Father give good gifts to those who ask him.'[3]

This idea was used (by Jesus or the Evangelists) not only to illustrate the fatherly character of God but to create a role-model or ideal citizen of the kingdom of God. Thus Jesus himself is reported to have welcomed children into his circle of followers.[4]

Throughout the following discussion there will be a conscious effort to avoid presuming any particular hypothesis of the dependence of one branch of tradition upon another. Without using language that reflects

2.   Cf. Vincent Taylor, *The Formation of the Gospel Tradition* (London: Macmillan and Co., 1964), p. 1: 'It is important that we should appreciate the distinction between the "Gospel tradition" and the Gospels. Before the Gospels were written the "tradition" was organic; it was a thing of life, and as such was always changing and growing'.

3.   Mt. 7.9-11. See Lk. 11.11-13. Luke apparently did not include the stone/bread line and instead has 'if asked for an egg would give a scorpion?'' following the snake/fish line. Also Luke identifies the gifts of the heavenly Father as 'the Holy Spirit'.

4.   Mt. 19.13-15 = Mk 10.13-16 = Lk. 18.15-17; Mt. 18.1-5 = Mk 9.33-37 = Lk. 9.46-48. See also *Gos. Thom.* 22, 46; cf. 37.

any theory of Gospel origins or relationships, it is clear that the theme of 'love of children' is to be found consistently in Matthew, Mark, Luke and John.

In the Matthean account of the request of James and John,[5] it is the mother of the young men who asks that a favor be given to her sons, namely, for them to sit on the right and left hand of Jesus in his kingdom.[6] While it is possible to suspect that Matthew has protected James and John as they are described in the Markan account,[7] at the very least it can be argued that Matthew's version of the story indicates that a mother was profoundly concerned about the stature and respect that her sons might receive within Jesus' kingdom.

Matthew, Mark and Luke all refer to the miracles of healing of Jairus's daughter and the boy with a spirit.[8] It is Mark and Luke, however, who seem especially to emphasize the theme of a parent's love for a child. Concerning the account of Jairus's daughter, Mark and Luke stress that Jairus begged Jesus to heal the girl—Mark using the phrase *parakalei auton polla*, Luke reporting *parekalei auton*.[9] Luke, further, identifies the girl as Jairus's *only* daughter.[10]

The idea of 'begging' is also present in the Lukan account of the healing of the boy with the spirit. In 9.38 and 9.40, Luke indicates that the father desperately pleaded on behalf of the child.[11] Thus again the Gospel tradition exhibits material that highlights the love that parents have for their children, love revealed in their wanting their offspring to be healed. In some instances the individual Evangelist seems to draw added attention to the details that enhance the dramatic qualities of the theme.

Matthew and Mark both report a pericope (which is not found in Luke nor in John) concerning a Canaanite or Syrophoenician woman and her child (Mt. 15.21-28 = Mk 7.24-30). Here Mark's account shows

5.   20.20-28. Found also in Mk 10.35-45 but missing from Luke and John.

6.   In Mark, 'glory' is used rather than 'kingdom'.

7.   Mark does not report any information regarding the mother of James and John. In Mark they make the request themselves.

8.   Mt. 9.18-26 = Mk 5.21-43 = Lk. 8.40-56; Mt. 17.24-31 = Mk 9.14-29 = Lk. 9.37-43a. Neither story is found in John.

9.   Matthew uses neither expression, employing the simple *legōn* and it is significant that in the Matthean report the girl is already dead.

10.   Matthew and Mark do not report this detail.

11.   The verb *deomai* is not found in Mark and only occurs once in Matthew in a passage he shares with Luke (Mt. 9.38 = Lk. 10.2).

an interest in the mother's love for her daughter. Matthew, on the other hand, seems to focus more on the woman herself, particularly in reporting her saying, 'Have mercy on *me*!' and in having Jesus praise the woman's *faith* which seems to justify or even make possible the miracle.

In the Infancy Narrative, Luke directs his attention to the theme of love of children shown by parents but, for our purposes, especially noteworthy is the Evangelist's awareness that Mary would experience anguish because of her son. Luke records that Simeon, in referring to Jesus and his divisive effect on people, told Mary: 'a sword will pierce your soul as well' (2.35).

Luke narrates the raising from the dead of a young man and describes the deceased as the *only* son of a widow (7.11-17). The dead man's life is restored because of the compassion of Jesus.[12] It may be assumed that the reader is to believe that Jesus (and perhaps Luke also) was sympathetic towards the widow because she was a grieving mother.

The parable in Lk. 15.11-32 focuses on a father's love for his sons, even for one who has deserted him. Verse 20 specifically mentions the father's compassion, and interestingly this is the very term used in 7.13. The original purpose of this story of the 'Prodigal Son' (whether Jesus' or Luke's) was to suggest the father-like character of God and the paternal compassion that embraces even those who might have turned from God. Thus Luke's theology is, to some degree, grounded in an awareness of parents' love for their children.

John's Gospel is dominated by the Father/Son terminology that early Christianity came to adopt in articulating the relationship between Jesus and God. There is, furthermore, clear evidence that the author made use of a tradition that testified to the devotion and affection that parents show towards their children. In 4.46-53 a father approaches Jesus with the request that his dying son be healed. With only a word of promise or assurance, Jesus performs the miracle. While the intention of this particular passage is to elaborate on the 'signs' Jesus performed (v. 54), it is evident from these examples that the different tributaries of Gospel tradition (that at some point were used by the separate Evangelists) echoed the theme of parents' love for their children.[13]

12. The verbal form of compassion *(splagchnizomai)* occurs in Lk. 7.13; 10.33 and 15.20. See also Mk 9.22.

13. In this connection it ought to be noted here that the claim in Mt. 10.37 = Lk. 14.26 is audacious.

b. *Jesus as God's Beloved Son*

It is obvious that the New Testament regards Jesus as the Son of God.[14] His status as the Son of God is recognized by the demons, implicitly acknowledged by Satan (Mk 3.11; Lk. 4.41; Mt. 4.3-6 = Lk. 4.3, 9); it is the confession of the disciples in Matthew (14.33; cf. 16.16), the insight of the centurion in Matthew and Mark (Mt. 27.54 = Mk 15.39), and the claim of Jesus in the Synoptic Gospels.[15] The Sonship of Jesus is emphatically claimed in the Gospel of John and this Christology is found throughout early Christian literature.[16]

The origin of the idea that Jesus is the Son of God probably derives from Jesus' own 'unique relationship with God, expressed in the address "Abba" "dear Father" '.[17] The further history of that development need not distract us. For our purposes it will be enough to show that an innocent person, believed to be God's Son, died a horrible death and cried out, 'My God, my God, why have you forsaken me?'

Not only does the tradition emphasize Jesus' intimate relationship with the God he called 'Father'. On a few occasions, Jesus is described as *a* or *the* 'beloved' Son (with whom God is pleased).[18] The origin of this designation might be found in the characterization of Isaac in Gen. 22.2, 12 and 16[19] or in the reference to the 'beloved son' in one of

14. Cf. the understated assertion of Oscar Cullmann, *The Christology of the New Testament* (Philadelphia: Westminster Press, 1959), p. 278: ' "Son of God" is indeed one of the means by which the first Christians expressed their own faith in Jesus'.

15. (Mt. 28.19?); Mt. 11.27 = Lk. 10.22; Mt. 24.36 = Mk 13.32.

16. E.g. Jn 3.16; 5.19-26; 10.36; Acts 13.33; Rom. 1.4, 9; 1 Cor. 1.9; 2 Cor. 1.19; Gal. 2.20; Eph. 4.13; Col. 1.13; Heb. 1.2, 5, 8; 4.14; 10.29; 1 Jn 1.3, 7; 2.22-23; 5.5, 9; Rev. 2.18; 1 Clem. 36.4; *Barnabas* 5.9, 11; 6.12; 7.2, 9; 12.8-10; *Didache* 7.1 (cf. 9.2-3; 10.2-3; 16.4); Ignatius, *Ephesians* 4.2; Ignatius, *Magnesians* 8.2; 13.1; Ignatius, *Romans* Intro; Ignatius, *Smyrneans* 1.1; Polycarp, *Philippians* 12.2; Hermas, *Similitude* 9.12.1-2, 8; 9.13.2-3, 5, 7; 17.1, 4; 18.4; *Mart. Pol.* 17.3; *Diognetus* 9.2; 10.2; 11.5; *Gos. Thom.* 44; *Gos. Pet.* 11.45-46; *Acts of Paul and Thecla* 6, 37, 42; *Apoc. Pet.* 1.

17. Martin Hengel, *The Son of God* (London: SCM Press, 1976), p. 63. Joachim Jeremias, *The Prayers of Jesus* (London: SCM Press, 1967), p. 65.

18. Mt. 3.17 = Mk 1.11 = Lk. 3.22; Mt. 17.5 = Mk 9.7 = Lk. 9.35 (in some MSS and other textual authorities); Col. 1.13; 2 Pet. 1.17; cf. Jn 3.35; 8.42; 10.17; 15.9; 17.23, 26; 1 Clem. 59.2-3; Ignatius, *Smyrnaeans* Intro.; *Barnabas* 3.6; 4.3, 8; Hermas, *Similitude* 9.12.5; *Mart. Pol.* 14.1; *Diognetus* 8.11.

19. Cf. Ernest Best, *The Temptation and the Passion* (Cambridge: Cambridge University Press, 1965), p. 169.

Jesus' parables.[20] Further, the address to Christians as 'beloved ones' could be part of this development.[21]

These issues also need not distract us from the central observation that early Christian literature regards Jesus as the beloved Son of God. Inasmuch as many of the Gospel traditions indicate that even imperfect human parents want the best for their children, it would seem that Jesus ought, therefore, to have enjoyed unparalleled blessing and protection as the Son of God. As might be expected within the Gospels, there are some suggestions that, like Zeus' care for Sarpedon until the fated moment, God 'warded off' (cf. *Iliad* 12.402-403) destruction from Jesus until the predetermined time for his dying.

The most significant text is Mt. 2.13-20 in which God, through dreams given to Joseph, guards the life of Jesus from those who seek to kill him (others include Lk. 4.30; Jn 7.30; 8.20). In the flight to and the 'exodus' from Egypt, Matthew finds a type of fulfilment of the prophet's apparent reference to Israel's experience: 'Out of Egypt I called my son'. Jesus, like Sarpedon, is 'kept safe' until his appointed hour (cf. Mt. 26.18, 45; Mk 14.35, 41; Jn 2.4; 7.6, 8, 30; 8.20; 13.1; 17.1).

It might be anticipated, then, that the beloved Son of God would in fact continue to know the protection of his Father and so be sheltered from pain or suffering even if death itself were somehow predestined, or at least prophesied. It is the mystery and the scandal of Christianity that it is 'God who delivers up his own Son' to be crucified.[22]

c. *Jesus as Forsaken*

Early Christian literature readily acknowledges (or proclaims) that Jesus suffered, was crucified and died a criminal's death.[23] While the

20. Mk 12.6 = Lk. 20.13. The adjective is not found in Matthew's version. See also Hermas, *Similitude* 5.2.6.

21. Cf. 1 Jn 3.1-2. For an overwhelming use of 'beloved' (*agapetoi*) in an early Christian writing, see 1 Clem. 1.1; (cf. 3.1;) 7.1; (cf. 8.5;) 12.8; 16.17; 21.1; 24.1-2; 35.1, 5; 36.1; 43.6; 47.6; 50.1, 5; 53.1; 56.2,16.

22. Frank J. Matera, *Passion Narratives and Gospel Theologies* (New York: Paulist Press, 1986), pp. 2, 23.

23. E.g. Mt. 27.31 = Mk 15.20; Lk. 23.33; Jn 19.16-18; Acts 2.23; Rom. 6.6; 1 Cor. 2.8; 2 Cor. 13.4; Gal. 3.1 (cf. *1 Clem.* 2.1); Phil. 2.8; Heb. 6.6; 12.2; Rev. 11.8; Ignatius, *Ephesians* 16.2; Ignatius, *Trallians* 9.1; Ignatius, *Philadelphians* 8.2; *Barnabas* 7.3, 9; (cf. Polycarp, *Philippians* 7.1). Cf. Joseph B. Tyson, *The Death of Jesus in Luke–Acts* (Columbia: University of South Carolina Press, 1986), p. 3: 'Although there are early documents that do not contain narratives about the

execution of the Son of God was a source of potential embarrassment and scandal,[24] the cross nevertheless became an ironic emblem of honor and glory.[25] John's Gospel seems almost oblivious to the implicit humiliation of Jesus' death, preferring to interpret it as an exaltation in being 'lifted up' (cf. 3.14-15; 8.28; 12.23, 31-33).

An integral part of the tradition is that Jesus endured the agony of crucifixion, dying an excruciating death. It was reasonable for the Docetists, whose attempt to protect the reputation of Jesus[26] was labelled 'heretical', to deny that the Son of God was literally and physically put to death on a cross.[27]

Matthew and Mark report that in his torment Jesus cried out with a loud voice,[28] 'My God, my God, why have you forsaken me?' Such a question on the lips of Jesus is a potential source of disillusioned perplexity for many,[29] and refuge is often taken in the assumption and belief that Jesus was merely beginning to quote or recite a passage from the Hebrew Scriptures. As a consequence, 'there is a temptation to empty the cry of abandonment of its content by drowning it in the optimism expressed in the conclusion of Psalm 22'.[30]

Without fully entering into the debate concerning whether the cry is (1) authentic as a word uttered by the historical Jesus, and (2) a genuine

crucifixion or even allusions to it, there still is evidence of a preponderant interest in it in the early church'.

24. 1 Cor.1.23; Hebrews 12.2; (cf. *1 Clem.* 16; Ignatius, *Ephesians* 18.1; Polycarp, *Philippians* 7.1; Justin, *Dialogue Trypho* 10.3; 90.1; Origen, *Contra Celsum* 2.9, 35, 68; 6.10, 34, 36.)

25. 1 Cor. 2.2; Gal. 6.14; Eph. 2.16; (cf. Ignatius, *Ephesians* 9.1; Ignatius, *Romans* 7.2; Ignatius, *Smyrnaeans* 1.1; *Gos. Pet.* 10.42).

26. Cf. Hengel, *Son of God*, p. 15: 'the most shameful death known to antiquity, death on a cross'. Martin Hengel, *Studies in Early Christology* (Edinburgh: T. & T. Clark, 1995), p. 363.

27. Cf. Martin Hengel, *Crucifixion* (Philadelphia: Fortress Press, 1977), pp. 15-21. Also, Hengel, *Studies*, p. 363.

28. *anebōesen...phōne megalē* (Mt. 27.46), *eboesen...phone megale* (Mk 15.34). Luke and John do not include this tradition but cf. the Gos. Pet., 5.19, 'the Lord screamed out (*aneboese*)'.

29. Thus those who argue that Luke used Mark's Gospel as a source often comment on the absence of the 'Cry' in Luke. Cf. Raymond E. Brown, *The Death of the Messiah* (2 vols.; New York: Doubleday, 1994), II, p. 73: 'The Marcan Jesus' citation of Ps. 22.2...would be intolerable in Luke's christology'.

30. Gerard Rosse, *The Cry of Jesus on the Cross* (New York: Paulist Press, 1987), pp. vii-viii.

expression of personal and immediate anguish, it may be observed that Matthew and Mark seem to present this saying as a real and empassioned outcry. In the other occasions where Jesus quotes the Scripture, even in speaking to the tempter Satan, Matthew and Mark consistently employ verbs that imply Jesus used simply a conversational voice.[31] By contrast, the cry of being forsaken is identified as being called out in a 'loud voice' and the mode of the cry is a scream.[32]

If it is suggested that a victim of crucifixion would be likely to use a 'loud voice' in speaking during the execution, and even cry out,[33] it seems highly unusual that Luke and John provide very little evidence to support such a claim.[34] Furthermore, Matthew and Mark certainly make no indication that the words screamed are a quotation from Psalm 22. Such an allusion is not recognized by the crowd who instead believe that Elijah is being summoned (Mt. 27.47 = Mk 15.35). Neither Matthew nor Mark regard the cry as a fulfillment or re-enactment of any Scripture or event in Israel's history. It seems apparent that, *at the very least*, the Evangelists intended their readers to believe that on the cross Jesus felt forsaken by God.[35]

2. God's Fatherly Testing of the Righteous

The principal interpretation of the suffering and death (and the apparent forsakenness) of Jesus in early Christian literature is that the crucifixion of the Son of God is the means of atonement for the world, that Jesus died for the sins of those who believe in him and that his death is a

---

31. Mt. 4.4, 7, 10; 11.7; 13.14-15; 15.3-9 (= Mk 7.6-7); 21.16, 42 (= Mk 12.1-11); 22.29-32 (= Mk 12.24-27); 22.37-39 (= Mk 12.28-31); 22.43-44 (= Mk 12.35-36); 26.31 (= Mk 14.27).

32. Loud voices are sometimes associated with those who are demon-possessed: Mk 1.26 (= Lk. 4.33); 5.7 (= Lk. 8.28).

33. Cf. Brown, *The Death*, II, p. 1044.

34. Cf., if original, Lk. 23.34 (*elegen*); 23.43 (*eipen*); 23.46 may offer some corroboration for the argument but even here Luke uses *eipen*. Cf. Brown, *The Death*, II, p. 1067: 'Mark's "to scream"…is too violent an action to be attributed to the Lucan Jesus'. Jn 19.26-27 (*legei*); 19.28 (*legei*); 19.30 (*eipen*).

35. Cf. Brown, *The Death*, II, p. 1045: 'Does the violent description of Jesus' outcry suggest that in his death struggle with evil he feels himself on the brink of defeat so that he must ask why God is not helping him?… There is much to encourage us to take it very literally at the level of the evangelists' portrayal of Jesus'. (Cf. p. 1051.)

sacrifice for his followers. The Letter to the Hebrews, however, identifies a number of 'secondary purposes' in the death of God's Son. One
of these is that Jesus, through the ordeal of suffering, was made perfect
and thus became empathetic with his followers in their time of testing.

> ...it was appropriate that the one for whom and by whom creation exists,
> in bringing his children to glory should make the pioneer of the chil-
> dren's salvation perfect through suffering (2.10).

> Because the children are flesh and blood, he took on the same nature in
> order that through death he might destroy the one who has the power of
> death, namely the devil,[36] and free those who are in lifelong bondage to
> the fear of death (2.14-15).

> And since he has himself suffered and been tested, he is able to assist
> those who are tested (2.18).

> In his body of flesh Jesus prayed and pleaded with loud cries and tears to
> the one able to save him from death. He was heard because of his rever-
> ence. Despite being a Son, he learned obedience through suffering and
> having been made perfect he became the source of everlasting salvation
> to all who listen to him (5.7-9).

Though necessarily inadequate (given the subject) some attention
must be directed to the idea of being made perfect, an idea perhaps
related to the theme of 'a righteousness which exceeds that of the
scribes and Pharisees' (cf. Mt. 5.20). The theme is certainly prominent
in Hebrews and it occurs in the Wisdom of Solomon (2.10; 5.9; [cf.
7.11, 19]; 7.28; 10.1; 11.40; [cf. 12.2]; 12.23; Wis. Sol. 4.13, 16). There
is a significant 'perfectionist' ethic in early Christian literature,[37] and
this standard of conduct may well have originated with the injunction to
be god-like in character and behavior.[38] Such a rigorous command,
seemingly impossible, is virtually a call to life out of death, demanding
the self-sacrifice of those who would follow.[39] In turn, this theme of

36. Significantly, in connection with the parallels to Wisdom of Solomon, this is
the only occurence of *diabolos* in Hebrews. See above, p. 64.

37. Many texts might be referred to but *Didache* 16.2 is one of the more dramatic.

38. Mt. 5.48 (cf. Lk. 6.35-36; Eph. 4.32-5.1; Ignatius, *Philadelphians* 7.2;
Diognetus 10.2-6).

39. Cf. Mt. 16.24-25 = Mk 8.34-35 = Lk. 9.23-24. The athlete imagery of
Hebrews and the theme of 'training' may be related to this idea of self-sacrifice in
the pursuit of perfection. It is very striking that Ignatius urged Polycarp to become a
'perfect athlete' (Ignatius, *Polycarp* 1.3; cf. 2.3; 3.1).

perfection would then provide some important background for the claim expressed in Hebrews that Jesus' death liberates the human children of God from the fear of mortality.

The 'perfectionist' theme in the New Testament is expressed in a bewildering, if not contradictory, form in 1 John:

> If we claim to be without sin we are self-deceived and the truth is not in us... If we claim we have not sinned, we make him a liar; his word is not in us (1.8, 10)... No one who abides in him sins; all who sin neither see nor know him... All who are born of God commit no sin for God's seed abides in them and because they are born of God, they are unable to sin (3.6, 9).

1 John, however, regards this strange transformation as a metaphorical resurrection: 'We know that we have passed from death into life' (3.14; cf. Jn 5.24). In some early Christian texts, baptism (kept undefiled) is understood to be the vehicle of that radical change (cf. *2 Clem.* 6.9; 7.6; 8.6; Hermas, *Similitude* 9.31.4).

The freedom from post-baptismal sin (which promotes the possibility of perfection) and the theme of new life in Christ is evident in Hermas, *Similitude* 9.16.2-3:

> 'It was necessary', he said, 'for them to come up through the water in order that they be made alive. For they could not enter the kingdom of God unless they put away the mortality of their previous lives. These who have "died" received the seal of the Son of God and entered the kingdom of God. For', he said, 'until a person bears the name of the Son of God, that person is dead. In receiving the seal, however, one puts away mortality and receives life' (Cf. also Rom. 6.1-3).

Within this expansive context it seems plausible that the author of Hebrews understood Christ to be able to sympathize with those who are tested because he was himself tested and likewise is empowered to free the children of God from the mortality that weakens their nature (and so make them 'perfect') because his own flesh and blood was liberated from a fearful subservience to death (thus making him 'perfect'). While such an emancipation is often, or even usually, possible only through physical death (which frequently entails martyrdom[40]), such 'perfection' might be achieved even in an earthly existence.[41]

---

40. Such is the apparent view in Wisdom of Solomon.
41. This significant development is found in early Christian literature.

The understanding of the death of Jesus and the consequent theodicy reflected in Hebrews seem to have been influenced by the Wisdom of Solomon. According to the letter, the suffering and testing Jesus endured were, to some degree, intended to make him a high priest able fully to empathize with his followers in their own suffering and testing. It is taken for granted, then, as in Wisdom of Solomon, that the children of God (i.e. the righteous) will in fact experience such ordeals. Interestingly, no protest is made as to why God would allow (or even cause) these to befall his sons and daughters.

About the righteous who are often tormented, Wisdom of Solomon (11.9-10a) claims that although they are:

> [d]isciplined [*paideuthentes*] a little, they will receive tremendous bless-
> ing because God tested them and found them worthy of himself. Like
> gold in a furnace, they were tried by him and like a burnt sacrificial
> offering he accepted them.[42]

This 'discipline' (*paideuomenoi*) is not a punishment but is instead a fatherly testing or warning (*noutheton*; cf. 1 Cor. 4.14). Hebrews, citing a text from Proverbs, echoes this understanding:

> Have you forgotten the encouragement which is spoken to you as
> children? 'My child, do not think so little of the Lord's discipline [*pai-
> deias*], and do not lose heart when corrected [*elegchomenos*; cf. Wis.
> 12.2] by him. For those loved by the Lord are disciplined [*paideuei*] and
> all accepted children are chastised.[43] You endure for the discipline [*pai-
> deiai*].You are being treated as God's children and what father does not
> discipline [*paideuei*] his child? If you are not disciplined [*paideias*], as
> all legitimate offspring are, then you are illegitimate, not God's child-
> ren.[44]

---

42. 3.5-6. The passage employs the verbs *peirazo* and *dokimazo*. Early Christian literature exhibits some reluctance to say that God 'tempts' but the idea of faith being tested (by God), sometimes with the goal of perfection in mind (!), seems to have remained acceptable (e.g. Jas 1.13-14; 1.2-4; 1 Pet. 1.6-7).

43. *mastigoi*. This is the only occurence of the term in Hebrews and it appears in quoting scripture. The author of the letter may have been uncomfortable with such a harsh word (cf. Wis. 12.22).

44. Heb. 12.5-8. Bearing in mind the athlete imagery of Hebrews, it is worth noting that this passage goes on to conclude, 'For the moment discipline is painful, not pleasurable, but in time, for those trained by it, it produces the peaceful fruit of righteousness'. For the theme of disciplining those who are loved, cf. Rev. 3.19.

3. *Conclusion*

This chapter has surveyed early Christian literature guided by the two themes of 'love of children' and 'the suffering and death of God's Son'. It is evident that the New Testament Gospels share the view emphasized in the *Iliad* and the Heracles tradition that parents are anxious for the well-being of their children. Further, like Sarpedon in the epic and Heracles in mythology, Jesus is regarded as the son of God. It is perplexing and frightening to find that, like Sarpedon and Heracles, Jesus is apparently abandoned by his Father and dies.

Early Christian literature (and Hebrews in particular for this chapter) asserts that the disciples and followers of Jesus are the children of God. Like their Master, they must suffer, often to the point of physical death. All believers, however, are involved in the contest (or struggle) to overcome the mortality that enslaves human nature. The question of the purpose of innocent suffering then becomes increasingly personal.

Hebrews finds an answer in the experience of Jesus and claims that Christians, like Jesus, endure suffering and testing in order to be made perfect through God's discipline. Adapting the scriptural framework of parental guidance and loosely employing the imagery of athletics, the author regards suffering not only as inevitable but valuable.

Chapter 8

CONCLUSION

Martin Hengel has claimed that when the Graeco-Roman world and Judaism both address an issue, the background of the topic for New Testament studies becomes 'particularly interesting'.[1] This is clearly true of the problem of innocent suffering. It is a theme that is common to several cultures and each has made a contribution which has influenced early Christianity. Here is further testimony that the Church was influenced by its setting in the Hellenistic society of the first-century Roman Empire.

Significant themes and characters have been considered in the *Iliad*, the Heracles tradition, Plato and Xenophon's portraits of Socrates, the Roman Stoics, the Wisdom of Solomon, and in early Christianity. All these sources have bluntly acknowledged the reality of undeserved suffering and have suggested various theological rationales. From the death of Sarpedon, the son of Zeus, to the execution of Jesus, the son of God, several attempts have been made to account for the misfortune of those who (presumably) ought to be protected by the supreme deity. This theme is dramatically presented in the Heracles story.

While Socrates is not referred to as the son of a god, his unjust sentencing to death raises the question whether piety, perhaps even perfection (according to human standards), often is ineffective and certainly unrewarded. The Roman Stoics interpret the issue on an individual level and seek to encourage virtue even in the midst of hardship. For them the athlete metaphor of rigorous exercise and God as the trainer for the Olympics provides a significant perspective on the problem of innocent suffering.

Wisdom of Solomon, while aware of such a view, prefers the interpretation that God is, like a father, testing or disciplining his children

---

1. Martin Hengel, *The Atonement* (Philadelphia: Fortress Press, 1981), p. 5.

through their suffering. Much of early Christian tradition and particularly the letter to the Hebrews embrace this theme.

The question, however, ultimately and painfully, becomes personal as the individual comes to ask in an immediate situation, 'My God, my God, why have you forsaken me?' While guesses and speculation may distract from the pain, ignorance stands ready to mock the inquirer. The researcher and the theologian may have any number of theories but perhaps it is only in the silence of faith and the peace of trust that God's answer can be heard. Still, the question must be asked.

BIBLIOGRAPHY

Arnim, H. von (ed.), *Stoicorum Veterum Fragmenta* (Stuttgart, 1964).

Aune, D.E., 'Heracles and Christ', in D. Balch, E. Ferguson, and W.A. Meeks, *Greeks, Romans and Christians* (Minneapolis: Fortress Press, 1990), pp. 3-19.

Barnes, H.E., *Hippolytus in Drama and Myth* (University of Nebraska Press, 1960).

Best, E., *The Temptation and the Passion* (Cambridge: Cambridge University Press, 1965).

Birley, A., *Marcus Aurelius* (Toronto: Little, Brown and Co., 1966).

Bonhoeffer, A., 'Epiktet und das Neue Testament', *Zeitschrift für die neutestamentliche Wissenschaft* 13 (1912), pp. 281-92.

Brown, R.E. *The Death of the Messiah* (2 vols.; New York: Doubleday, 1994).

Campbell, R., *Seneca: Letters from a Stoic* (Harmondsworth: Penguin Books, 1982).

Cullmann, O., *The Christology of the New Testament* (Philadelphia:Westminster Press, 1959).

Easterling, P.E., *Trachiniae* (Cambridge: Cambridge University Press, 1982).

Finan, T., 'The Myth of the Innocent Sufferer: Some Greek Paradigms', *Proceedings of the Irish Biblical Association* 9 (1985), pp. 121-35.

Frend, W.H.C., *Martyrdom and Persecution in the Early Church* (Garden City, NY: Doubleday, 1967).

Garrison, R., *The Graeco-Roman Context of Early Christian Literature* (Sheffield: Sheffield Academic Press, 1998).

Grant, R.M., *The Apostolic Fathers* (6 vols.; London: Thomas Nelson and Sons, 1966).

Greene, W.C., *Moira* (New York: Harper and Row, 1944).

Grene, D., and R. Lattimore (eds.), *Euripides*, III (Chicago: University of Chicago Press, 1959).

Hengel, M., *The Atonement* (Philadelphia: Fortress Press, 1981).

—*Crucifixion* (Philadelphia: Fortress Press, 1977).

—*The Son of God* (London: SCM Press, 1976).

—*Studies in Early Christology* (Edinburgh: T. & T. Clark, 1995).

Hogan, J.C., *A Commentary on the Plays of Sophocles* (Carbondale: Southern Illinois University Press, 1991).

Hoistad, R., *Cynic Hero and Cynic King* (Lund: C.W.K. Gleerup, 1948).

Hick, J., *Evil and the God of Love* (Norfolk: Macmillan and Co., 1966).

Horbury, W., and B. McNeil (eds.), *Suffering and Martyrdom in the New Testament* (Cambridge: Cambridge University Press, 1981).

Jeremias, J., *New Testament Theology*, I (London: SCM Press, 1975).

—*The Prayers of Jesus* (London: SCM Press, 1967).

Kagan, D., *The Peace of Nicias and the Sicilian Expedition* (Ithaca: Cornell University Press, 1981).

Knox, W.L., 'The "Divine Hero" Christology in the New Testament', *Harvard Theological Review* 41 (1948), pp. 229-49.

Kolarcik, M., *The Ambiguity of Death in the Book of Wisdom 1–6* (Rome: Pontifical Biblical Institute, 1991).

Kreeft, P., *Making Sense Out of Suffering* (Ann Arbor: Servant Books, 1986).

Kushner, H.S., *When Bad Things Happen to Good People* (New York: Schocken Books, 1981).

Leibniz, G.W., *Theodicy* (trans. E.M. Huggard; ed. and abridged by Diogenes Allen; Don Mills, Ontario: Bobbs-Merrill Co. Inc., 1966).

Lutz, C.E., 'Musonius Rufus: "The Roman Socrates" ', *YCS* 10 (1947), pp. 3-147.

Malherbe, A., *Moral Exhortation: A Greco-Roman Sourcebook* (Philadelphia: Westminster Press, 1989).

—*Paul and the Popular Philosophers* (Minneapolis: Fortress Press, 1989).

Matera, F.J., *Passion Narratives and Gospel Theologies* (New York: Paulist Press, 1986).

Metzger, B.M., *The Canon of the New Testament* (Oxford: Clarendon Press, 1987).

Mikalson, J.D., *Honor Thy Gods* (Chapel Hill: University of North Carolina Press, 1991).

—'Unanswered Prayers in Greek Tragedy', *Journal of Hellenic Studies* 109 (1989), pp. 81-98.

—'Zeus the Father and Heracles the Son in Tragedy', *Transactions of the American Philological Association* 116 (1986), pp. 89-98.

Moseley, N., *Characters and Epithets* (Yale: Yale University Press, 1926).

Most, G.W., 'A Cock for Asclepius', *Classical Quarterly* 43 (1993), pp. 96-111.

Oldfather, W.A. (ed.), *Epictetus* (2 vols.; Cambridge, MA: Harvard University Press, 1967).

Pfister, F., 'Herakles und Christus', *Archiv für Religionswissenschaft* 34 (1937), pp. 42-60.

Rad, G. von, *Old Testament Theology*, I (2 vols.; New York: Harper and Row, 1962).

Rose, H.J., 'Herakles and the Gospels', *Harvard Theological Review* 31 (1938), pp. 113-42.

Rosse, G., *The Cry of Jesus on the Cross* (New York: Paulist Press, 1987).

Russell, J.B., *Satan* (Ithaca: Cornell University Press, 1981).

Schein, S.L., *The Mortal Hero* (Berkeley: University of California Press, 1984).

Schoedel, W.R., *The Apostolic Fathers*, V (London: Thomas Nelson and Sons, 1967).

Scullard, H.H., *From the Gracchi to Nero* (London: Methuen, 1976).

Sevenster, J.N. *Paul and Seneca* (Leiden: E.J. Brill, 1961).

Talbert, C.H., *Learning through Suffering* (Collegeville: Liturgical Press, 1991).

Taylor, V. *The Formation of the Gospel Tradition* (London: Macmillan, 1964).

Tyson, J.B., *The Death of Jesus in Luke–Acts* (Columbia: University of South Carolina Press, 1986).

Wender, D., *Hesiod and Theognis* (Introduction and Translation) (Harmondsworth: Penguin Books, 1973).

Williams, C.K. and Dickerson, G.W., *Sophocles: Women of Trachis* (New York: Oxford University Press, 1978).

Williams, S.K., *Jesus' Death as Saving Event* (Missoula, MT: Scholars Press, 1975).

Winston, D., *The Wisdom of Solomon* (Garden City, NY: Doubleday, 1979)

INDEXES

INDEX OF REFERENCES

OLD TESTAMENT

OTHER ANCIENT SOURCES

INDEX OF AUTHORS

THE BIBLICAL SEMINAR